Hey mom, I think I might be good at writing.
One day, I think I'll write a book."
-John Marshall Foster 2015

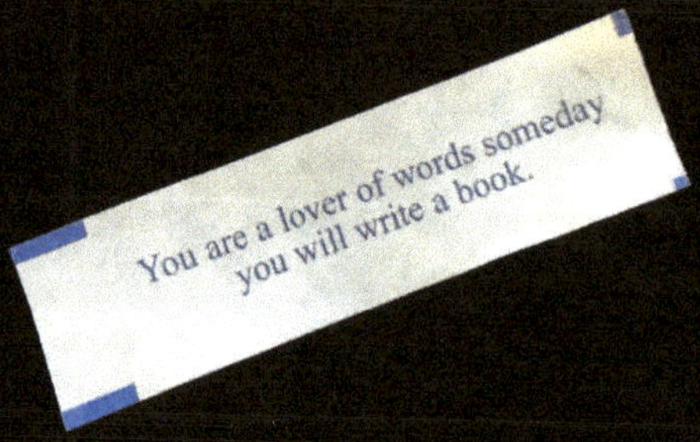

Found inside Marshall's locked box.

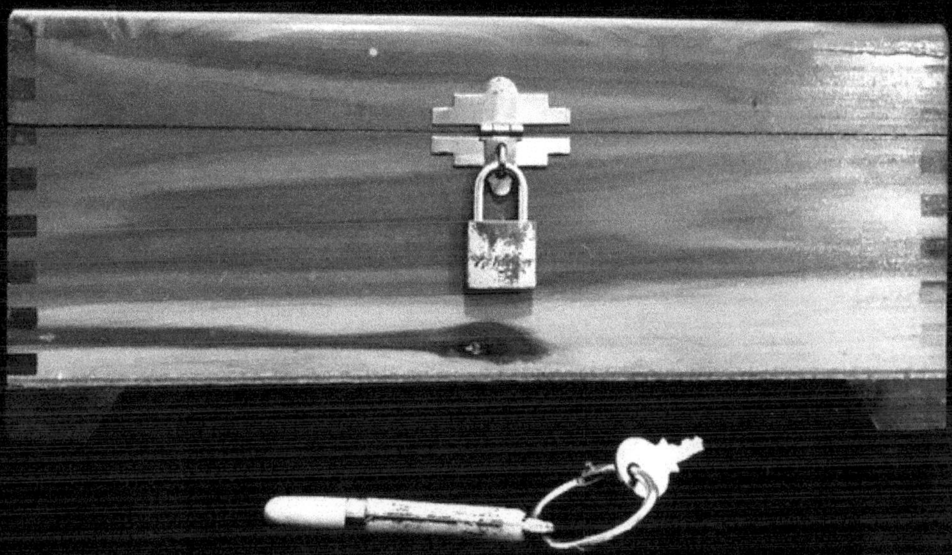

Marshall's Locked Box

DEDICATION

To my four children
and all other brave warrior Ordinary Angels
who tirelessly impact positive changes

INSIDE HIS

locked BOX:

The Marshall Racing Project 33 Story

Susan E Foster

Clovercroft Publishing

Inside His Locked Box

Published by Clovercroft Publishing, Franklin, Tennessee

Published in association with Larry Carpenter of Christian Book Services, LLC
www.christianbookservices.com

Edited by Gail Fallen and Michelle Vardeman Martin

Copy Edit and proofread by Gail Fallen

Cover and Interior Design by Suzanne Lawing and Diana Chang

Printed in the United States of America

Hardcover ISBN: 978-1-954437-09-8
Trade Paperback ISBN: 978-1-954437-08-1

This book was written by Susan E Foster in her personal capacity. The personal accountings, opinions, and views expressed in this book are the author's own and do not necessarily reflect the views of the Tarrant County Hospital District d/b/a JPS Health Network.

Author's Note: This book was written by Susan E Foster based on true stories. Some names have been changed and some stories altered. The personal accountings, opinons, and views expressed in this book are the author's own and do not necessarily reflect the views of any other individual or entity mentioned in this book. Stories mentioned are common or classic to what many experience. Any situation described in this book that may be similar to those of others is a matter of pure coincidence.

CONTENTS

Ever Gomez, founder of the Marshall Racing Project 33

FOREWORD

ABOUT THE MARSHALL RACING PROJECT 33

The Marshall Racing Project 33 (MRP33) is a movement born from the death of a 21-year-old young man named Marshall Foster, who committed suicide following his miraculous survival of a harrowing motorcycle accident. It was not the accident that led him to end his life. It goes much deeper. Marshall was battling thoughts of suicide long before the crash.

In her second book, *Inside His locked Box: The Marshall Racing Project 33*, Susan E Foster gives voice to her late son, John Marshall Foster. It is an extraordinary story involving John Peter Smith Hospital in Fort Worth, Texas, and Trauma 1 Unit Nurse Ever Gomez, who forged an unconventional friendship with Marshall during his recovery when they discovered a shared passion for speed and motorcycle racing.

Marshall experienced perhaps his greatest sense of joy, accomplishment, and independence on the seat of his motorcycle, a black Kawasaki Ninja. It was so much more than a motorcycle. It was a dream realized, a symbol that he had made it. It was also the exact same model Ever was riding at the time.

During Marshall's extensive hospital recovery period, Ever visited Marshall often. He offered to help him sell or repair his crushed motorcycle while also inspiring hope in a young man who was suffering from a broken soul and a loss of aspiration for the future. Their friendship continued to flourish when Marshall was finally discharged from the hospital. Together they met to discuss their motorcycles and how they could ride together.

What Ever did not know was that Marshall was battling thoughts of suicide . . . and had been long before the motorcycle crash. Marshall was trying, once more, to rebuild his life. It was something he had faced many times before—fleeing domestic abuse, moving to new homes, attending new schools, leaving friends behind, starting all over again. But this time, he didn't make it.

After Marshall's passing on October 12, 2017, Marshall's mother was scrolling through his text messages and came across conversations between Marshall and Ever. She immediately contacted Ever to offer him the wreckage of Marshall's motorcycle for parts, and Ever accepted.

What followed was the launch of The Marshall Racing Project 33 (MRP33), a special event arranged by Ever on behalf of mental health awareness and to surprise Marshall's family and friends with the unveiling of his completely refurbished bike painted in his

Ever racing Marshall's completely refurbished Kawasaki painted in Marshall's favorite color, green, featuring the number 33–Marshall's birthday, March 3rd.

favorite color green featuring the number 33 representing Marshall's birthday, March 3.

Reborn from the tragedy of suicide, Ever transformed Marshall's broken dream into a beacon of hope delivering the important message that when you feel most hopeless, you are positioned for your coming breakthrough. Ever and Marshall's story is a reminder that although we may not see it, there is always reason for hope and life matters. Your life matters.

Since then, MRP33 has teamed up with The Jordan Elizabeth Harris Foundation to help bring continued awareness to HOPE SQUAD, a peer-to-peer suicide prevention training program for elementary, junior high, and high school students. And with generous funding from The Tara Sawyer Foundation, Marshall's Ordinary Angel, Ever, and MRP33 are empowered to expand and grow this important message of hope.

In this book, Marshall's words, his "reflections" as he called them—school assignments, short essays, and personal notes—are sprinkled throughout. Marshall didn't push through to the other side of his darkness, but Susan's family hopes that sharing his story, along with the words of others who uniquely understood his struggle, will inspire hope in anyone grappling with mental illness and the eternal questions of life.

This is Marshall's story and, critically, the story of too many more. According to the United Health Foundation, "Nationally, the suicide rate increased 25.4 percent from 1999 to 2016, with increases occurring in every state, save for Nevada. In 2017, there were an estimated 1.4 million suicide attempts and more than 47,000 deaths by suicide, making it the tenth leading cause of death in the United States. Firearms were involved in half of all suicides and there were more than twice as many deaths by suicide than by homicide."[1]

Now, through a series of revealing conversations, text messages, and essays written by her son, Susan shares an in-depth and profound look inside his life. From his own written words, readers will learn what triggered Marshall's journey while also highlighting what his mother and siblings endured during a very difficult and tumultuous time in their lives.

-Cindy Birne, Cindy Birne PR

**A portion of this book's net sales proceeds go to The Marshall Racing Project 33 (MRP33), benefiting mental health awareness.*

PART 1

It's John not Marshall

I was born with the name John Marshall Foster. People call me Marshall. People call me John. And some people like to call me Foster. Ever since kindergarten I have liked the name Marshall. But why does my grandpa call me John Marshall? My coach calls me foster, as well as, my football team mates. But why do people call me John and not Marshall? I have been the new kid at school many times and I have to tell them my real name is John but I like Marshall more. All my new teachers call me John.

"I hate him," Marshall, my then 12-year-old son said.

"Oh, be careful of hate," I cautioned him. "Hating leaves your own soul bruised and does nothing to him."

"Why is he so mean?" Marshall continued.

"Hate is how he got where he is," I replied. "He has enough self-hate for all of us."

"Then why does he always brag about how holy, righteous, and good he is if he hates himself as you say?" he asked.

Marshall was my little truth seeker, always seeking to understand and know the truth.

"I don't think he hates himself at all," he argued. "He loves himself . . . *a lot*!

"I see what Dad is doing," Marshall firmly decreed at the ripe young age of 12. "He gets us to work, promising us things, but he never follows through," he continued, listing off all his father's broken promises. "I see how he works, and I'm going to tell him."

"Oh God, no, Marshall," I said in what I hoped was my best persuasive manner. "Marshall, please don't. You are not able to handle the backlash that will come from it. I *agree* with you, but keep it to yourself, for now. It is not safe for you to confront him like this. You're too young. Trust me."

Marshall had no idea all that I had protected him from emotionally. I would often say to my husband I shouldn't have to be my children's PR agent to their own father. Their father, Seth, was continually coming to me with complaints and accusations he wanted to confront them about. I'd manage to divert his attention or take the blame for their perceived infractions, enticing him to hurl his insults at me instead of them.

The most insidious tool an abusive parent uses to prop up their feeble ego is their own child. Their full knowledge that the innate, innocent trusting nature of a child longs to believe the love and intentions of a parent are good, true, sincere, and worthy of trust is the very vulnerability they feast upon rather than protect. As a cat plays with their food, a "bully" parent toys with the need their children possess to *feel* loved by them. Children are pawns to use and manipulate, as their ego hungers for empowerment. This abuse will continue as long as the child allows it, even into adulthood. Therefore, children of these toxic parents are at risk of substance abuse, suicide, and other mental health issues. Likewise, children of abusers are also some of the most intuitive, aware, wise, and emotionally intelligent adults around.

* * *

Upon my realization there was no stopping Marshall, I said, "If I can't stop you, I'm going with you."

"The more you see, the more you let yourself see, the more you realize that you can't go back into ignorance and unsee what you've already seen. You have two options. One is to set yourself on fire with anger and let it burn you into cinders and ash. And the second is using the fire of that anger to get into action."[1]
—Beth Martens

"Go do it. Go make a mistake, go fail. Take a chance. Take a risk. Do something that's sure to make your fears come up. That way, you'll get past them, fast! Put yourself out there for somebody to criticize you, so you can see how great you are."
—Beth Martens

"Fine," he said. His determination obviously had the best of him. "I'm going now."

And with that, he briskly walked past me down our winding staircase with his small shoulders squared like a soldier going into battle.

On the way, I shared with his sister Sophia what he was doing.

"Oh, no . . . Mom!" she said, as she, too, tried to discourage him. Determined, with his mind made up, Marshall marched on, dismissing both our pleas to reconsider.

Narcissistic parents have an ego fragile as a bomb. They rarely admit wrong even when faced with facts and damning evidence. In fact, being faced with the truth of their wrong will likely set them into rage. For the sake of appearances, they may offer a disingenuous acceptance of some small, insignificant infraction as if to say, "See, I admit wrong when I am wrong." They never stop lying and often resort to what I have since learned professionals refer to as "gaslighting." They guilt trip and twist the truth, forcing the victim to apologize to the abuser for that which the "toxic" abuser is guilty. And that was the exact sick, twisted response Marshall received from his father that day. It brutally undercut Marshall's trust in his own reality and sense of self.

Throughout the couple of hours during which Marshall was made to stand while his dad sat tearing down his young son's worth and value, accusing him of being spoiled, lazy, and unappreciative rather than owning his accused habit of broken promises made to the kids as reward for their work, Sophia stood outside the window showing her brother support. With their father's back facing her, she stood looking into Marshall's eyes. Seth twisted the truth about himself, projecting his own guilt upon Marshall, accusing him of being selfish, ungrateful, disobedient, and rebellious, topping it off with "You are a loser," demanding Marshall apologize, admitting the guilt of which he himself was guilty. I finally called him off.

Marshall's direct confrontation with truth birthed a quiet raging flame within his father that would not *ever* be extinguished.

"That's enough!" I said, ending the tirade. Seth's willingness to end it at my request without any backlash against me suggested he knew he had crossed a line.

"Marshall never fully recovered from that episode," Sophia would later say.

She was right. Years later, Marshall revealed he could never get out of his head that his dad called him a *loser*.

"I see a champion in you. Who do you see?" I would often say.

"You say that to all of us," he'd say, repelling my compliment.

Marshall with his younger sister. They were a team.

I try to treat girls nice, too,
and will straighten out a guy who doesn't.
That makes me real mad.
-Marshall

"That's true. But I say it for four very different reasons," I'd insist.

Talking truth, love, affirmation of Marshall's thoughts, feelings, and observations, I tried to steady him emotionally from his own father's blow.

I call these abusers, *Charming Impossibles.* Charm is their lure, and impossible to please is their method of manipulation and control. Once a Charming Impossible dumps their dark accusatory anger on another, they become "light." They become giddy, fun, and enjoyably light-heartedly charismatic. This is what Seth did after dumping rage and other emotional venom upon any one of us.

Following the episode with Marshall, Seth gathered the family for fun at the basketball hoop. Marshall was deeply emotionally wounded. The projection and twisting of half-truths is designed to cause victims to second-guess themselves, creating a lack of trust in their own intuition. It utterly breaks them. And that's exactly what happened to Marshall that day.

While Marshall spun in mental anguish, with no time to process, Seth required him to join the family in a "fun" game of basketball, expecting laughter and fun from all, taunting and teasing anyone who was not "showing" feelings of being "happy." Very similar to a scene in the movie The Great Santini, it was as though he was playing out his inspiration from a VHS he brought home for us to watch years prior. "The character in this movie reminds me of me," he admitted, comparing himself to Santini for all of us to hear.

Thinking at the time that it was a lucid moment of self-realization and hope for change, I now deduce it was more a warning. I only wish I had listened. Like all of Santini's family members, we, too, learned how to go along with plastered smiles on our faces because faking it was better than the alternative. If he was in a good mood, we all were supposed to be. If he was mad, he wanted us to be mad too.

In *Confessions of a Sociopath*, M. E. Thomas explains how Charming Impossibles don't feel as others do. They learn how to act as though they feel by watching others.3 We learned how to perform the emotions he wanted to see in us to temporarily appease him. Fortunately, he couldn't see through our smiling performance, although we all clearly did, eyeing one another encouraging each other along until the charade was over.

Eventually, we'd go into our separate rooms to unravel the chaos: how we truly felt, what we really thought, and what was actually happening . . . and why. But before we had time enough to process it, much less discuss it, Seth would create more drama. It could be anything from the crisis of not purchasing the right toilet paper to using the wrong spoon to stir the contents of a saucepan. "If I want anything done right around here, I have to do it myself!" was his war cry. And just like that, we were off one crisis and on to the next. Having multiple mixed-up episodes of drama and twisted accusations all at the same time was our crazy, mixed-up, insane life behind beautiful doors.

Following Marshall's devastating emotional blow from his father, I began getting calls from the school counselor as Marshall developed behavioral issues we had not previously seen, further exposing the emotional wounds from that fateful day. And behavioral issues at school were just what Seth needed to hammer down more on the audacity of his son confronting him, our great family leader, the priest of our home, he who could only be reproved by God himself.

With Seth's fragile ego now challenged by his own son, our home life grew continually darker. Narcissistic sociopaths go for the jugular when threatened by a minion stepping out of line even when that "minion" is their own child. Seth was losing power over his family. His control and dominion had been (in his mind) brazenly challenged, so he cowardly attacked his youngest son. Marshall cracked open a hornet's nest, bringing on himself full-on vengeance. Seth continued his campaign to reclaim dominion over his family by making an example of Marshall, threatening anyone else from attempting to step out of line as he did. One such punishment for getting in trouble at school was making Marshall sleep with the dogs.

Marshall's realization of the discrepancies in his father came at a huge cost to all of us, but especially to him.

Pet Peeves

Do you know that person who brags about what he will say to a cop or to another person because he thinks he can say whatever he wants to anyone? But then five minutes later when that same braggart faces that particular person they were just talking about, when that same person is walking right towards you and you challenge the braggart to start talking to the person like they said they would, what happens? For some reason, they always have an excuse why they can't say what they said they would. That is one of my pet peeves that really just bothers me. Grow some balls and say what you said you would when that person is in front of you or just leave your comments to yourself.

Another thing that just crawls under my skin is being late periodically. It doesn't help you or anyone else. One reason I hate being late is because my dad made me late to almost every single event I had planned. I would tell him to leave one hour or thirty minutes early and I was still showing up late to where I was going. So now I get really stressed when people are late unless there's a good reason. If you ever have to take me somewhere or go with me somewhere, be on time or you will get on my nerves.

This is something else that drives me crazy, too... people judging others on how they look or act. If you don't know someone and you don't know what their lives are like then I would suggest you don't judge them because you have no clue what they have been through or what they are capable of. I will admit that I judge people sometimes but at least I try to think of what they have been through and stop myself from judging. I hope I don't catch anyone judging someone they don't know or I might have a few words to say right back at their face.

Last thing that I have to say is that if you're the person who's annoyed by people who are just trying to have a little fun. Why do you have to be so negative about people having fun? Sometimes it goes too far with immaturity but at least be a little more positive so life can be more enjoyable for you and everyone around you. Life is what you make it. All you have to do is choose to be happy- or not.

-Marshall

At 12 years of age, my son would have to sleep outside with the dogs, in the cold, for a week. Walking away from him, leaving him alone nightly, crying alone, left a deep scar in both our hearts. We each cried silently, separately, privately . . . and alone. Most often than not, the tears never even came. Too accustomed to the belittling for crying (because tears were made fun of), we cried dry tears.

"The dogs are kind, Marshall," I would remind him. "They are beautiful and loving. The only one true beast is the monster living inside, your dad."

Defending my children directly to their dad only brought on more verbal abuse toward them. Running to their defense only caused a torrential outpouring of wrath and rage . . . upon them.

"You are 'mama's boys,'" Seth would relentlessly tease my sons. "You poor little babies need your mommy to defend you. Waaahhh!" He'd laugh and taunt them like a schoolyard bully.

This cyclical torment that periodically surfaced with growing, compounding vengeance was cause for me to rip myself from my son's side each night, leaving him outside in his sleeping bag with Duchess, our Great Dane. It wasn't so much the act of making Marshall sleep outside as it was the insidious nature of how he was ordered outside, stripping away at Marshall's worth, suggesting he didn't deserve to sleep in the house, digging at his sense of self-worth rather than a poor choice in actions. My efforts to divert abuse or defend the children became risky for all of us. Realizing any effort to protect them would only bring on even more taunting from their dad toward them, I said, "Let me know when you are ready to leave, Marshall. Let's get out of here!"

"I'm seventy-five percent ready," he replied after sleeping several nights outside.

"Let me know when you are one-hundred percent. I'm ready to leave when you are, but I will not leave one of you behind. Just say when you're ready."

* * *

Recent new studies show that ADHD in children is often rooted in anxiety and anger.4 Therefore, when ADHD is suspected or diagnosed in children, many schools and medical professionals are looking into what is causing the anger before prescribing medication or other therapies. Anger is a secondary emotion to a primary emotion (such as hurt) and often presents itself in learning disabilities. Marshall suffered learning challenges and was diagnosed with ADHD. He took medicine for one month, but didn't like the side effects. Marshall was angry, very angry.

Abuse causes a rewiring in the brain. Marshall had all the signs of PTSD. At the time, I didn't know that. It was only later that I learned this from a counselor.

"You think suicide is cowardly? I'll tell you what's cowardly. Hurting someone so much that they want to end their lives. That's cowardly."
—Author Unknown

Hot Summer Days

The house we live in has been flooded 5 times but my dad still wants it. We clean it out every time but this time it got above the second floor. It was destroyed internally. But my father believed we could fix anything so we had to clean and fix the house up once again. It was my friend's birthday party and I told my dad that the party started at 3:30pm when it really started at 5. He's always late so I wanted to be on time. But wait, my dad cares about himself and his house. We worked at his house every other day of our summer but just this once he wouldn't let me go to that party. I wanted to make my best friends party but my dad said I need to work more, it was hard slave labor.

-Marshall

Our river house that flooded multiple times

After this episode with his father and several visits to the school counselor, Marshall emotionally shut down. He closed himself off to everyone as if he had made a pact with himself not to talk . . . at *all* . . . about *anything*. I asked my then 13-year-old to read a book on anger and write about it. Hoping to help him not only understand himself, I hoped it would help him express himself and relieve the ticking time bomb he'd become. Marshall, my child who hated reading and rarely wrote, to my shock, actually read the book and filled an entire lined notebook page with words in pencil. This is what he wrote:

It makes me angry to read this book because I don't want to have to read about anger that makes me more mad, and if I'm angry when I do homework, I won't be able to do it or I will do bad and make a bad grade. I can't read when I'm angry! One of the reasons I have rebellion is because when I was little, anything that happened I kept and 1 little thing that hurts will hurt 3X more now. There are five steps to rebellion and they are being hurt in your heart, bitterness, Anger, stubbornness and rebellion, and all three steps lead to now from the past. I have been angry for a long time and I have wanted to kill myself, but my friends called me and changed my life and they told me how it would change theyre life drematicly and I really didn't want to hurt my best friends. I wanted them to feel that I care about them and that I loved them. I love all my friends and if we fight I will always get back with them.

"Look, Mommy! It's me and you in front of our house. See my big muscles?"

The house we fled. Our Great Dane, Duchess, and cat, Jag, are in the front yard.

Making friends didn't come easy for Marshall. From kindergarten through adulthood, even into his professional life, he'd come to me for advice on how to go about making friends. When he was young, his anger would get in his way. In his adulthood, he simply didn't know what was acceptable. Consequently, he suffered tremendous loneliness all his years of growing up. In his scrapbook, I found a card I colored with his markers stating, "Be patient, God has special friends for you."

At 20, working with men older than he, he'd discover they'd verbally jab at each other with friendly teasing, bantering back and forth in "man talk," the way many men do. It's a fraternal male bantering in jest that he didn't understand.

"C'mon, Marshall," they'd egg him on, inviting him to jab back. "C'mon, Marshall, give it back to us," they would say, basically inviting him into relationship, friendship.

"Mom, should I?" he asked me one day. "Should I really jab back at 'em?" he asked. "I don't know what to do."

Marshall had come to me his whole life for advice on friendship. He didn't know how to joke around with a bunch of guys because the only teasing in our family was directed from Seth toward one of us . . . and it was "fun" only to one: Seth. And Seth would not tolerate the least sarcastic comment, even if it was said in jest. He was heavy on doling it out, and it always led to hurt. In our home, teasing was yet another form of abuse, which is why Marshall had no concept of how to interact with those adult men in friendly back-and-forth banter.

For Marshall to have finally developed a network of friends he mentioned in his note was huge in his life. He wanted and longed for friends of his own so badly and finally was developing a support group all his own at a critical time in his young life.

In March 2010, those same kids mentioned in his note contacted me to have a surprise birthday party for Marshall in our home. This was a first! I had never experienced him having such a beautiful support group of friends, nor did I know these kids or their parents, as Marshall had attended a new school that year. They were nice, what I had always hoped for him. They, along with a couple of their moms, brought a cake, streamers, posters, and food, complete with a plan on how to surprise him. It was precious, meaningful, and very significant in his time of great pain. To peel him away from that was tough to consider.

Not even a month later, on April 1 of that year, we left. Pulling himself from that group of budding friendships was deeply, deeply wounding and a great case for why abusers should be jerked from their homes rather than victims having to flee. An emotional wound from leaving friends was as deep, if not deeper, than those he suffered from leaving his father.

Marshall had already shut down from facing his father, and after leaving all his friends and support system in addition, Marshall went mute. For a while, Marshall completely turned off. He couldn't talk. He could barely even get a complete of sentences out, even to me. His wounds ran so deep.

We Chose What Was Right

I was with my brother at Dicks Sport Store and we were finally leaving with his friend who just got off work. Then my brother got a call from my mom and saying she's coming to us right now, don't move. She got to us and told me to get in the car and I did. I saw her talking to my brother wondering what it was? It had to be important. She told me to come out and said were moving out tonight to Dallas. And we did. As soon as we left, I couldn't find my phone charger but I knew it was in my houses yard. So, we went back not knowing if my dad would show up from his business trip. I got it and we were told to never pick up his phone call for a while.

-Marshall

I later learned this is what Charming Impossibles do. It's part of their crazy, chaotic cycle. It's classic. Evidently, they can transfer their darkness onto someone else in order to lighten themselves. And this is what happened almost every time with Seth, no matter which of us was his chosen emotional dumpster. This specific episode with Marshall; however, became pivotal in our family. Things changed after this. Everyone had become of age and was able to see, recognize, and disagree with what was going on. And we became very concerned for Marshall, our youngest and most vulnerable, developing what a retired abuse counseling expert from The Family Place in Dallas years later called the strongest "trauma bond" she had ever seen in her career.

Sandy was a counselor willing to see us as a family. Because we were all adults, most counselors insisted on seeing us individually. As a family going to counseling together, we learned that trauma bonds form when the victim develops a twisted attachment to the abuser, first accepting blame, then being accused of enjoying it.

Uniquely, our common bond linking us together was of being mutual victims. Sandy explained to us how we were linked by an unbreakable chain that most likely saved us as well. "All Seth wanted," she said, "is to snatch just one of you into his clutches. Just one was all he needed.

"This should be a case study," she added. "In my thirty-seven years of practice, never have I seen a more insidious, manipulative shredding and stripping every fiber of your foundation out from under you."

She was especially intrigued how he used our faith to sabotage us. Her validation that for us, faith held us hostage rather than set us free (as further confirmation that our trauma bond saved us), helped us during the long journey ahead requiring diligent unraveling so that we could each be free to live our own lives. Unfortunately, I didn't learn about all this until much later.

Mom, are you sure Dad can't come take me from you?
I talk to a girl who has to go to her Dad every summer
even though she doesn't want to. She's 14, too.
-Marshall

Why do people call her that?

Hey look at the girl with the big stomach. Everyone says she has sex with anyone who dates her in the summer because she's always pregnant on the first day of school. Everyone called her a slut, even her friends. But why is she crying alone in the back of class in my health class? I started talking to her and getting to know her, because I just felt I needed to. It's summer now and we hang out every week but I felt I needed to ask about her baby. I found out she was pregnant because she goes to her father who made her have sex with his friend. I wondered why she was getting big again.

-Marshall

Not all of Seth's self-loathing was turned upon Marshall. The others had an equal share. We all did. I was continually cleaning up his emotional messes with all four of my children on top of my own. He was tireless in his destructive rampages. He never seemed to rest from the outpouring of abuse. And yet we couldn't see it because he mixed in delightful, unexpected surprises like a family meal at a favorite seafood restaurant or a "fun" adventure ride in the evening fog on our horses.

His constant pounding at one of us was relentless, but so were his fun family nights watching the National Geographic Channel. Also mixed in were exotic family sailing trips in the Virgin Islands. Our experiences were all over the place. From the outside looking in, one could easily wonder about what on earth we could complain. Of course, we were constantly reminded of that, and our blessings were certainly many. It was confusing.

A Family Vacation

I awake with the smell of salty water and fresh wind. I found myself on a boat. Not a motor boat a sail boat. The sounds of splashing water and a flapping sail soothed me back to sleep. Once again I wake up but not to the same sounds. It sounds like an explosion? I opened my eyes seeing a dark cloudy sky. With curiosity, I asked what is going to happen? My father seemed stressed. He told me to go down inside. The boat started to move more violently than usual. The best thing I could do is sleep but why was the boat tilting side to side violently?

-Marshall

PART 2

"Now, every time I witness a strong person,
I want to know: What dark did you conquer in your story?
Mountains do not rise without earthquakes."
—Katherine Mackenett

While away in Colorado, I received a call from Marshall.

"Mom, I'm okay, but I had a motorcycle accident and I'm about to go in for surgery," he said, his words echoing into my soul trying to awaken comprehension and gravity.

"Marshall, is there a nurse around?"

"Hello?" answered a harried, intense female voice.

"Ma'am, is this a matter of life and death?" I asked, dread gripping my soul.

"Um, Marshall . . ." she said in a shaky, high-pitched voice, "do you have any final words for your mother?"

"Mom, I appreciate you. I love you."

"I love you, too, Mar—" Click.

I love being scared. I'm not sure why but
it makes me happy to feel the adrenaline.
-Marshall

Looking out the sliding glass door to the Beaver Creek snowcapped mountain miles and miles away from JPS Hospital in Fort Worth where my 20-year-old son was headed to surgery all alone, I stood grasping for thoughts and emotions. I felt nothing. Empty. Frozen. My mind traversed to exactly a month prior sitting with the family at the dinner table for Marshall's twentieth birthday dinner party, waiting on him because he was uncharacteristically late. He was late because he came on his new Kawasaki Ninja "crotch rocket" as he affectionately referred to it. It was an all-black motorcycle he had just purchased that very afternoon.

"Another thing that just crawls under my skin is being late periodically. It doesn't help you or anyone else. One reason I hate being late is because my dad made me late to almost every single event I had planned. I would tell him to leave one hour or thirty minutes early and I was still showing up late to where I was going. So now I get really stressed when people are late unless there's a good reason. If you ever have to take me somewhere or go with me somewhere, be on time or you will get on my nerves."

-Marshall

"Don't judge me if I don't stop my life to take care of you!" I announced before the whole family at Marshall's birthday celebration dinner.

So this is how he's going to try to end his life, was my first thought knowing Marshall struggled with not wanting to live. Something we all struggled with, at times, but his had become more deeply concerning.

My second thought was, *No, God won't let him die like this. He just wouldn't. But I fear the condition in which He may allow Marshall to live. Please, not somehow permanently impaired, oh God, no, please: that would be even greater hell on earth for him!* How do I allow myself to even think such things?

"Don't judge me if I don't stop my life to care for you one day," I told him over birthday cake when he told us about his new motorcycle.

Marshall is holding back his secret in this photo. He had just purchased his bike but we didn't know it yet.

"Mom! Stop! I can't believe you just said that!" was the unanimous response from my other children.

"I'm sorry," I said quieting myself.

But I wasn't. I knew the immature, inexperienced, crazy, reckless boy driver he was. I also knew the angry, frustrated, hanging-on-by-a-thin-thread, wonderful, tender, sensitive, hurting son that he was. None of which was a healthy mentality to be riding a powerful Kawasaki Ninja "crotch rocket" as he so sentimentally referred to it.

We all went out to see the beauty, his pride and joy. And beautiful, it was! It really was very nice.

Looking brand new, Marshall fought back a huge grin; he was proud of himself, as he so should have been. Having saved his money over the past couple years, he bought it in full with cash, put himself through a riding class, and secured a motorcycle driver's license and insurance without telling any of us. His twentieth birthday gift to himself was our surprise.

We all oohed and ahhed over it. It was impressive.

At the close of the evening, Aunt Gaye asked that he spend the night.

"It's dark now, Marshall. Will you please stay the night and leave in the morning?" He agreed.

"Marshall, I really am very proud of you," I later told him. "I've always taught you to dream big and that you can accomplish anything you put your mind to. You have dreamed of having this since you were a little boy."

"It's all I've ever wanted, Mom," he responded. "I did it myself!"

"You did, indeed. And I'm very proud and happy for you."

His calls became more positive.

"Mom, I'm making new friends with other guys who have bikes, the kind of friends I've been wanting to get to know. This bike is really turning things around for me, Mom. It's good. Really good," he said. "Things are looking up," he added, in an effort to reassure me.

"I'm happy for you, son," I reiterated. "I am very pleased. It's nice to hear you so happy."

One month later, almost to the exact date of his birthday dinner party, while in Colorado, I received that life-altering call. His call to me left me in silence. I stood in absolute silence. It was as if time stopped. I then group texted his siblings to inform them of what little I knew.

They all gathered in the emergency waiting room, waiting for any news. I waited from afar. Finally, the silence breaks. Marshall is in the ICU. He can't see visitors. The children stay in the waiting room. Uncle Arthur and Aunt Gaye go to join them followed by my friend, Gina. I wait. Sound stopped again. Silence overwhelmed me. I didn't dare to think. Scolding myself, how *dare* I not think.

I didn't know what to think.

My two very best friends had sent their daughters on to heaven. *One at 10 years of age, the other at 15. Was I to send mine at*

20? Stop thinking like that! He will be fine. He will be fine.

I called Dr. Jay Haynes, medical director of the hospital. He let me know that with HIPAA laws, it could take a while to learn about Marshall's case but that he would inquire and get back to me as soon as possible.

Gina calls. She says, "Come home. Your son needs you."

Still no sound. Only every other word from voices and only the directives from the words. Otherwise, like a character in a silent black and white movie, I function.

On a packed 5:00 a.m. shuttle to Denver International Airport, my phone rings. It's Dr. Haynes.

"You are on your way home, right?" he says.

My heart beating through my chest, I realize that he's talking to me like a doctor, not a friend. *Oh God, no,* I think to myself. His tone is unusually professional. I don't like the implication of that.

"It's a miracle, Susan!" he says, "It's a miracle your son is alive. I am amazed at and so proud of our staff. Dr. Gandhi saved Marshall's life. Do you hear me?"

Yes, I heard . . . rapid speed, no other vehicle involved, internal bleeding, ruptured spleen. Rated from one to five, he now is a four. He is stable. Broken bones and appendages. But not worrying about broken bones, right now. Many die monthly from this in our hospital. Friend's young daughter hit a tree skiing and died on way to hospital due to ruptured spleen. Minutes from his life passing. But he's here. Must stabilize before concerning ourselves with other injuries, no brain or spinal injury. It's a miracle.

Don't Show Off Too Much

We were on the Costa Rica beach with 4 wheelers all to ourselves. But I had to ride with the instructor because I was too young. After a few laps I kept asking the instructor to ride with me to show him I'm good. After we got to a private stop on the beach, then the instructor let me drive a lot. I was so excited to be able to drive alone. I tried to get my brother's attention by yelling but the engines were too loud. Ouch! I was being burned and I started hearing steam. I looked down and found myself in the ocean on a 4 wheeler with the instructor behind me. Don't show off too much.

-Marshall

Finally arriving back in Texas, I make my way to Marshall's room. I see smiling faces. Peace. Calm. All the family is there. Gina is there. Marshall is out of ICU and in a private room. He looks wrapped like a mummy on one side, with machines and patches attached all over his chest. He's barely clad in a thin hospital gown with a white sheet disheveled and crumpled by his feet. He's smiling and says, "I thought you weren't going to change your life for me."

We grin.

My young adults have been taking care of one another for days before I arrive. They have a system and it's working great. Nurses seem more like aunts and uncles, they know my kids so well. A wonderful system is in place. Taking comfort in the confidence my young adult children exude, I rest and watch.

It was good. Very good.

Audrey and I spent nights there together with him in his room. With her returning to work, I stayed nights with him myself. One day while Marshall was at the end of his recovery at the hospital, I realized he was becoming his old self again. I said to Nurse Lisa, "I'm going home tonight and leaving him with you."

"Good," she said, "I got this."

I knew she did.

"Please make sure he *never* comes in here like this again," I implored.

"I sure will," she said, adding, "This is *nice* Nurse Lisa. I *can* be mean. And he certainly doesn't want to come back to *mean* Nurse Lisa!"

Perfect. I went home leaving my son behind with not only peace but also anticipation of so much more goodness happening in my son's heart and soul for his much-improved general well-being. A miracle took place that they all saw, were so very proud of, and came to his bedside to see. But there was another miracle equally monumental taking place in him that they couldn't see. It could only be seen from a mother's vantage point. With that said, any mother understands what I mean. It was good. It was so very good. Marshall was beginning to see that there was a purpose in his life being spared. Much of the staff who came to see him would tell him so.

This advertisement featuring Marshall was on billboards, in magazines, and on Taco Bell tray covers.

That cliff I jumped

I like the rush of falling out of the sky. It's a tingle that gives me adrenaline. I love being scared. I'm not sure why but it makes me happy to feel the adrenaline. After a few times of jumping off the cliff I remember looking back and seeing my friend holding a fire cracker. It was a black cat. After I fell in to the deep water it took forever to get back up to breathe some air. But as soon as I looked up out of the water my friend threw the fire cracker in the water and I could feel the push of the pressure in the water. It was a fun experience.

-Marshall

Toward the end of Marshall's recovery, the police officer who tended to Marshall the day of his accident called me to see how Marshall was doing.

Marshall arriving at San Diego airport on a friend's trip.

"You were part of a miracle," I said, adding how Marshall's life was miraculously spared.

"There's more to that miracle," the officer replied. He explained that the 911 callers who stopped beside the road at the scene of Marshall's accident directed emergency crews to the wrong highway. They guided first responders to Business 187 just as I drove past the described scene on Highway 187. Had I not been right where I was at the time of the call, I would have missed it, and help would have arrived 30 minutes or more later.

"It was a miracle I was there," he said.

A few orthopedic surgeries later, Marshall was put back together for an expected full 100-percent recovery, finally released, able to return to his apartment. He could go home, but it would be several months before he could return to work. The Marshall I took to his apartment after several weeks of surgeries and recovery was an even stronger and more confident young man than the Marshall who entered that hospital one month after his birthday. He exuded personal growth in uniquely crucial ways. He had been sincerely nurtured by the staff.

Due to the miraculous nature of Marshall's recovery involving JPS and the community Trauma 1 emergency system, he was asked to speak about his experience before the Texas State Legislature in Austin.

On July 13, 2016, The House Appropriations Committee's Subcommittee on Article II and the House Public Health Committee held a joint hearing regarding the interim charge to study the Texas Trauma System. Over the course of four hours, testimony was given by the Department of State Health Services, emergency care providers, physicians, and allied healthcare providers on the Texas Trauma System. Marshall gave testimony before the joint committee hearing on his own personal experience with the Texas Trauma System. He told his story of what had happened to him just a few months earlier, expressing thankfulness that he was taken to a major trauma center where life-saving interventions and specially trained medical personnel were readily available to care for him. He answered questions the committee asked, was passionate in sharing his story, and eager to have a positive impact on the legislative session and the decisions that would be made regarding his state's Trauma System.

Marshall was recognized by many of the top medical and legislative professionals for presenting one of the most articulate and impactful testimonies they'd ever heard. They

credited him for their decision to provide funding that was at risk.

The Marshall I had brought here only six years prior could not look anyone in the eye and was almost mute, hardly able to talk, he was so emotionally collapsed. Marshall had come a long way. JPS played a significant role in his emotional development.

As I celebrated joy for each of my kids and their courageous rebuilding of themselves, another dark cloud hovered in the distance.

Texas State Legislature Talk Description July 13, 2016

The House Appropriations Committee's Subcommittee on Article II and the House Public Health Committee held a joint hearing regarding the interim charge to study the Texas Trauma System. Over the course of four hours, testimony was given by the Department of State Health Services, Emergency Care Providers, Physicians, and allied healthcare providers about the Texas Trauma System. I gave testimony before the joint committee hearing on my own personal experience with the Texas Trauma System. I told my story of what happened to me just a few months earlier. I expressed thankfulness that I was taken to a major trauma center where life-saving interventions and specially trained medical personnel were readily available to care for me. I answered questions the committee asked. I was passionate in sharing my story, eager to have a positive impact on the legislative session, and the decisions that will be made regarding my state's Trauma System.

-Marshall

Mary Ann's Story

When I met him, Marshall was recovering after he had been discharged from our trauma one center. He was unassuming, gentle, and soft-spoken. The wounds from his motorcycle crash were still visible and healing. In thinking about that first encounter, what strikes me now was his welcoming smile and gentle handshake.

At the time when I came to know Marshall, the Texas Legislature was preparing an inquiry to report on the state's Trauma System. This report would reflect finance, service delivery, planning, and coordination among EMS providers, Regional Trauma Advisory Councils, and trauma centers. They wanted to identify strengths and weaknesses of the trauma system, reduce any redundancies in services, and build on the coordination of services to advance the delivery of trauma care in the state of Texas. With the way Marshall was so responsible in wanting to do everything to recover and pay his hospital bills, Marshall represented hope to me. I knew his burden was heavy, yet his eyes showed tenderness and acceptance. As a registered nurse working in a Level 1 trauma center for many years, my role has changed from emergency and critical care bedside nursing to a role of injury prevention. In the course of my work, there are several key strategies to reduce both intentional and unintentional injury. Strengthening individual knowledge, building coalitions, and influencing policy have been shown have impactful approaches to injury prevention. But talking about a recent near-death experience can be very up-regulating and highly influential. Therefore, I asked Marshall and his mother, Susan, if they would like to share their experiences regarding Marshall's care in the trauma center by testifying before the Texas House Appropriations and Public Health Subcommittees that were studying the Texas Trauma System. They both agreed by signing up through me. We met in Austin the night before the committee meeting and talked about what we thought would transpire the following day.

The State Capitol is beautiful and awe inspiring. It is the largest State Capitol in the US, and even taller than the Capitol in Washington, DC. It is true, everything is bigger in Texas. The rotunda is a magnificent circular room with paintings of former Texas governors and past presidents hanging on the curved walls. There is an incredible echo in the space that makes your voice sound like it is booming from a microphone. This was clearly evident as we walked through the Capitol together. By entering this historic building, we each sensed the importance of what we were a part.

Both Susan and Marshall had prepared notes for their testimony. I was excited, too. We arrived at the designated room. It was impressive. Twenty members of the House Subcommittee were ensconced on a dais facing a room overflowing with physicians, members from the Department of State Health Services, nurses, regional trauma council chairs, medical directors, emergency medical technicians, paramedics, members from the Texas Trauma and Acute Care Foundation, hospital administrators, trauma surgeons, concerned community members and, of course, Susan and Marshall Foster. We were all a bit nervous.

We three listened to hours of discussions from the committee surrounding many things related to trauma and disaster care, providers, readiness, sustainable funding, and many other details regarding the State's Trauma System. It was all very formal. Testimony was given from the perspectives of the multidisciplinary teams of trauma care providers in the room. The House Subcommittee asked specific questions surrounding the processes of the Trauma System, regulation, funding, and general operational queries. After all the technical details were reviewed, Marshall and Susan were asked to share their story. Marshall walked to his seat confidently and bravely.

The room went quiet when Marshall and Susan spoke before the House Subcommittee. Marshall was obviously the youngest person there. Susan sat by his side as he spoke with the most humble and grateful attitude. He introduced his mother and himself and said he was just starting his adult life when the motorcycle crash occurred. He shared some memory of the event, sure to mention that he had been wearing a helmet. He talked about going very, very fast, about separating from the bike, finally coming to rest on the ground. He remembered being "picked up" by ground EMS. He remembered the pain from the "road rash" over his arms and back. Breathing was painful, too, from the fractured ribs. He told the committee of his broken leg, the open fracture on his arm, and a deep pain in his abdomen that was caused by a ruptured spleen. His injuries were life threatening.

Marshall spoke so gently about the care he received from the medics when they transported him to the trauma center. He expressed heartfelt thankfulness at the care he received while in the hospital. He talked about the doctors and nurses and how much he valued their tender care. He was so glad to be alive. He recognized the potential impact he possessed by telling others of his miraculous recovery.

Eloquently expressing his desire to give back, to be able to "do his part" by offering affirming words of gratitude to the people who had cared for him, his presentation to the policy makers was a clear picture of his experience as a patient who was well-cared-for within the Texas Trauma System. How he boldly represented himself was impressive. To be so young, he was tasked with much.

When he finished giving his testimony, there was pause in the room. His whole-hearted words caused us to reflect on what is important in life, how important family is, and how very much he loved his. Marshall's testimony strongly impacted the decisions being made that day.

Marshall's testimony contributed to the committee's support of the Texas Trauma System. I am honored to have witnessed his hearing and to have spent time with him. I am thankful for his passing through my life and for Susan, who is also brave. As she champions spreading awareness about mental health and suicide prevention while supporting Level 1 Trauma Centers of Texas, I know Marshall is watching over her and all of us with his gentle smile.

Many people don't know how organized the state's trauma system is. Not all states are as well-funded and equipped. We, as Texans, are very fortunate. Precise rules, standards of care, regulations, and accrediting organizations making sure best practices and evidence-informed care are delivered from the scene of the injury and during transport, to time in the trauma bay, operating room, ICU, step-down units, and even rehabilitation floors, are strictly followed. This system helps to ensure optimal patient outcomes and reduces the chances of death. If you are injured and taken to a Level 1 Trauma Center, your odds of surviving are increased by 25 percent versus receiving care at a non-designated hospital.

In my years of advocacy work informing our policymakers about violence and injury, I have learned that trauma is the number one cause of death in ages one to 44.[1] I work to let policy staffers know that alcohol and substance abuse impacts judgment and that about half of all admitted trauma patients are positive for one or both of those conditions.[2] I let them know that injury and violence costs the US $840 billion a year and that for every one dollar invested in youth suicide prevention, $43 are saved, as well as many lives.[3] I also tell them that suicide is the second most-common reason a young person dies in our state.[4] Motor vehicle crashes are the first.[5] Throughout this crucial presentation of prevention statistics and evidence-informed initiatives, however, it is the personal accounting of someone's experience that truly gets the point across. Marshall got his point across *for us* that day.

—Mary Ann Contreras, RN

Violence and Injury Prevention Manager, Trauma Services

JPS Health Network

With over 30 years' experience as a nurse specializing in the field of trauma, emergency, and critical care, Mary Ann currently serves as a violence and injury prevention manager at JPS Health Network, the Level 1 Trauma Center in Fort Worth, Texas. Mary Ann studies trauma, behavior, environment, and policy to develop, implement, and evaluate prevention initiatives. This involves multidisciplinary coalition work focusing on prevention and improving the communities we serve. She is also involved in professional education of trauma healthcare providers, advocating and educating for proficient care of patients in trauma centers and within trauma systems. Mary Ann strongly believes positive community change is influenced by strengthening individual knowledge, promoting community and provider education, fostering coalitions and networks, changing organizational practices, and influencing policy and legislation.

Mary Ann Contreras RN was named 2020 JPS Outstanding Healthcare Advocate

Three Objects Presentation

Attention! My name is Marshall Foster and for about the next three minutes I am going to share with you what is significant to me about the following three objects: a set of ear phones, a teddy bear and a motor cycle. I would appreciate your undivided attention while I share with you how these three objects represent me.

The first object I chose was my pair of ear phones. The reason ear phones is an object that represents me from my perspective is because I love to listen to people and embrace their feelings especially when they are stressed and need to let out anger or hurt. I like helping people with their problems by being able to be there for them. I have always told my friends to text me when they are stressed or have some personal problems because I will try to help them with their situation. I also like it when people actually listen to me with understanding and without interrupting me when I am talking. I think people

This is the toy Marshall held up that day. He kept it on his dresser for years for motivation to one day achieve his dream. It just so happens that it is a replica of Ever's first motorcycle: same make, model, style, and color.

should wait their turn respectfully and I try to do the same for others, as well. So if anyone needs to talk to me, please tell me.

Other people that I have asked about my personality said I was apparently huggable and they suggested that my second object should be a teddy bear. I was told I am tall. I am 6' 3" which isn't so tall but I was also called "fluffy" and it was also said about me that I was a friendly person. With this I could agree. I try to be the person that everyone likes. While it's impossible to make everyone happy, I like bringing peace around me.

My last and final object has to do with what my future will look like and what I want to do. So of course I chose a toy motorcycle but it resembles a large life size street bike.

The reason I chose it is because I want my life to be dangerous. I want that adrenaline rush and stories to tell about my amazing adventures and actions. Motorcycles are dangerous for any use but I really don't care about my safety. I just want to live my life without worry and if I die?... Then I die having lived a worthwhile life. I want to be proud of what I do like sky diving, bungie jumping and so many other similar things that people are scared of. Because people fear pain or death, they are scared, live under stress and are worried all the time. I just want to live life.

In conclusion, I know that I want to use the life that I have and not waste it with fearfulness, guiltiness and regret. I will be proud of everything I do so I don't let those little situations or problems ruin my day. If you ever feel like life will never get better just think of how much worse it could be and know that there are always other people who have lives way worse than yours.

-Marshall

* * *

Ever since Marshall was 12, he struggled with life, the meaning of life, questioning if he wanted to live. Since leaving, we all faced those challenges. Life was heavy, dark, and kept beating at us with ferocious force. While Marshall recovered at home alone, he spent considerable time feeding his addiction to video games. He began sinking back into depression. He told the mother of one of his friends that he felt like a failure for having wrecked his motorcycle. He told her he felt like a loser, a comment from long ago that kept circulating in his mind.

After an accident of that magnitude, it is common for the most mentally healthy person to suffer depression. It's a common response, one to monitor no matter the mental health of an individual. But the pile-up of issues began weighing Marshall down.

"I don't belong here. I don't want to be here," he would more frequently say. "I would never want to bring children into this hell. If I go now, I hurt fewer people," he'd say, trying to convince me. "Mom, please . . . you are the only reason I'm still here . . . I need you to be okay with this."

"No," I'd say, "No, never Marshall. Stop this. Please."

One day he informed me he was on a 21-day water fast. I was not quite sure what he hoped to accomplish from this. It involved careful juicing and trying natural, healthy specific foods before reintroducing regular meals back into his system. While I didn't understand his purpose, the interest and care for his health seemed positive to me. He was *trying* . . . trying *something*.

"Mom, I need you to be okay with this, please," he'd more frequently beg me. "I'm done, Mom, let me go."

"No! Never! You can't do this, Marshall!" I'd insist. "We'll find you help," I'd say.

Counselors, programs, self-discovery training, new career training . . . he tried it all, only to say, "Mom, are you finished yet? Are you done?"

"Go see the movie *The Shack* with me," I asked, grasping for new strategy.

"Oh my God, Mom! I don't *feel* like going to see a movie."

"The least you can do is go to a movie with your mother if you're telling me you're leaving me!"

"Oh-my-God-Mom!" That was one word to Marshall. I heard it plenty. To really drive home his point, he'd break it down, "Oh . . . my . . . God . . . Mom!"

"There are only meaningful struggles, not meaningless ones. You can give meaning and purpose to life by first extracting the truth and separating the pure from the impure, the you from the not you. It's an act of bravery because people are attached to even the worst things within themselves."[6]
—Beth Martens

"So what did you think about the movie?" I asked on our way home from *The Shack.*

"It'd be nice if it were true," he answered. "I just don't know what is true, and I want to know."

Marshall would call every week or two to hash out his questions about life, death, God, faith, truth, friends, masturbation, jobs, drug use, sex, girls, how shy he is, his dreams, broken dreams, and why his breath stinks.

There really wasn't much I didn't know about him.

His friends would tell me stories they thought I had surely not heard. Most, I had. He talked to me about everything. On one hand, he wore me out. On the other hand, I love how he trusted me with some of his deepest thoughts, questions, and insecurities. It was unusually intimate, precious, and very sacred because he was extremely private and rarely trusted anyone.

With him, everyone was guilty, fake, and a liar until proven honest and trustworthy. Everyone would be put through a rigorous study and few, if any, were so entrusted as was I. But I knew that one wrong move, one statement spoken as truth that couldn't be verified, one white lie revealed, and he'd never trust me again. I had to be very careful and thoughtful in how I responded to his questions.

Thankfully, he kept coming back. The pressure of his burden to know and understand concepts even Socrates didn't know left him disgruntled. And it kept me up at night, pacing the floors. He was a beautiful 20-year-old son calling his mother weekly for deep hour or hour-and-a-half discussions seeking truth, what is real about God and why we are here. He was my son. He reminded me of the young me seeking a supernatural experience with God, with that same tenacious spirit insisting on receiving knowledge in an *I have to know* determination lacking the same maturity and understanding as I. He was a "mini me" but with an *or else* attached. An *or else I'll go and find out my own way* kind of attachment.

"You expect too much of yourself," I'd tell Marshall. "You are twenty-one going on seventeen. You are immature partly due to having been through so much. Give yourself a break. Some of these questions are not meant to be known on this side of life. Accept your humanity and its limitations. We don't know what we don't know."

"I gotta know the truth," Marshall would retort.

"Well, good luck with that!" I once said in exasperation. "There are how many religions in this world? How many factions within each religion? Within each faction, you could ask people on the same pew what they believe is true, and you'll hear them dissect the same passages to support both sides of an argument. We don't know. It's a personal process. You must come to your own truth that you can accept. That requires living, experiencing life, time, and developing your own true life experience with God, your creator!"

Silence.

I hoped he heard me.

"Come stay with me," I suggested. "Get out of your apartment and spend a week with me. We'll exercise, get outside and walk, breath in fresh air, and work on you."

Marshall's wrecked motorcycle—what felt like to him a death of a dream. "Mom, please take me to see my motorcycle." That was his first request upon leaving his month plus stay at the hospital. Sliding open the metal door of his storage unit, Marshall hoisted himself from his wheelchair, hopping on one foot, to embrace his bike in desperate plea, asking, "Why, why, why . . .?" It was all he could say draping himself over his bike, hugging it in anguish.

Finally, he agreed. Finally, I had hope. I talked with Gina and others about activities and things we could do. But the day he was to come, he called.

"I'm not coming."

There was no talking him into it.

Then he stopped answering my texts. I'd call Winston to text him. "Please make sure he's alive. I need to know he's alive."

"Mom, he isn't going to do anything. We're all miserable, but we'll push through. We always do. He won't really do it," Winston would reassure me.

"He's fine," Winston would later text to confirm.

My heart would calm, at least enough for a decent night's sleep.

Marshall's wrecked motorcycle—what felt like to him a death of a dream. "Mom, please take me to see my motorcycle." That was his first request upon leaving his month plus stay at the hospital. Sliding open the metal door of his storage unit, Marshall hoisted himself from his wheelchair, hopping on one foot, to embrace his bike in desperate plea, asking, "Why, why, why . . .?" It was all he could say draping himself over his bike, hugging it in anguish.

There is a vulnerability we expose ourselves to when we chase after our own dreams. The fear of failing at our own dream is greater than any other failure. Because what do we do when we feel we have failed at achieving our dream? What else is there to live for? Especially when you suffer from seeing things in stark black and white, as Marshall and I do. Learning to see hues and other beautiful colors takes time with people like us. Would he give himself time?

In reading about the many people who have achieved their dreams, we learn most fail many times and in multiple ways on the road to success. While at the cusp of breaking through to the next level in our lives, we always must anticipate a great battle. They seem to come right before every breakthrough. That's when we must fight the temptation to quit. In his book *The Dream Giver,* Bruce Wilkinson calls these challenges "Border Bullies."7 They fight us at the precipice of every new breakthrough.

Marshall was in what I call the "breakers" of life. It's kind of like in the waves in the ocean that crash one after another after another. He was fighting feelings of failure having literally wrecked his dream, but he was also engaged in the often unknown psychological battles that come with traumatic accidents and a foundation of childhood trauma.

In this moment of emotional instability, still suffering from inability to concentrate and focus and other childhood trauma-related issues, he decided to initiate a complete career change. That can mentally challenge even the healthiest of minds.

Why I want a Career in Public Safety and Why I Should Be Selected in this program

by Marshall Foster

Protecting others and looking out for those who can't defend themselves has always been a role I find myself in where kids at school are concerned and even in other circles of people, including my own family. I am the youngest of my family but am also the biggest. People seem to have always expected more from me because I am larger and stronger. I guess that makes me look older. But they also respect me more, too. Some guys would use that to run over others or take advantage of others. Kids can be pretty mean to each other. I have been treated that way myself by my own father. So, I try to do differently. I try to be nice to the kid everyone else makes fun of. I can without being teased because I am big and kids won't mess with me. And I try to treat girls nice, too, and will straighten out a guy who doesn't. That makes me real mad.

When I heard about this program, it was the first time I got really excited about any career idea or concept. My mom took me to meet a friend of hers who started out his career in firefighting and he got me even more excited. I have had a difficult family life and have been in six different schools since the fifth grade. So, it has been hard to keep friends. I like the idea that fire fighters have a close bond of friendship kind of like what I see happens in the military. This opportunity gave me hope when I was beginning to lose hope. I really need this chance. I hope you will consider me. If you will give me this chance, I will prove to you that I was the right choice.

* * *

"Mom, I can't do this job another day," he said one day. "It's stressing me out. I can't remember what to do. I can't focus, I can't do it anymore."

Looking back, Marshall had been showing signs of PTSD even before his accident.

Marshall was an installer for AT&T. After several months on leave recovering, his return to work stressed him severely. Derailed emotionally, he could no longer handle the technical job. The pile-up of childhood circumstances, divorce, and strained relations with his father and grandfather threatened his sense of worth. Probable injury to his brain no one had yet considered along with emotional trauma that often accompanies serious life-threatening collisions was likely another obstacle to his well-being. These factors combined with his lack of concentration and ability to focus caused him to start shutting down.

Marshall's return to work was on a feeble foundation. Even more challenging was his determination to quit his job, forcing himself into starting a new career path (a heavy load even for a healthy soul). He was slowly becoming buried under the weight of it all, plus the pile-up of debt from his leave and medical bills. I helped him financially with what I could. He met with Mary Ann from JPS, who was able to assist him in creating an affordable payment plan. Because that stressed him, he shoved aside the plan and paid off every medical bill, in full. Paying those bills was very important to him. Paying that debt devastated him financially. He was spiraling down . . . and fast.

"Marshall, you are creative and enjoy working with your hands," I'd tell him when discussing other options for him to consider.

"I'd like welding, I think," he said numerous times.

Then came the call for help: "Mom, I quit my job today. I'm done."

Oh my God! He is in real crisis, now.

It threw both of us into deep turmoil. Marshall prided himself on making a good salary, his independence, sense of responsibility, and taking good care of his finances and belongings. He needed a plan and fast!

When I was in crisis, the Women's Center of Tarrant County offered me excellent professional instruction, training, and direction. Remembering that men were also in my class, I called to ask about their current services. The woman I spoke with read me a list of their services and education programs. She mentioned a work-training program where grant money had been donated to help people learn certain skills. Local businesses collaborated with the Women's Center students to provide them jobs upon successful completion of their training.

"Please list the areas in skill training," I said. "Computer, medical, welding—" she read from a list. "Welding?! Did you say welding?" I interrupted.

They provided welding training! I couldn't believe it! The application deadline was the next day. If accepted, Marshall would be required to pay $150. The other expenses were covered through generous donations and grants.

"Marshall, have I great news for you!" I said when I called with the news.

Marshall was proud to work for AT&T in the beginning. As his emotional state plummeted, he struggled to concentrate, and his regular routine became more difficult for him. I now know he was showing signs of PTSD and most likely he suffered brain trauma from the wreck as well.

"Mom, there must be a catch because I know how much it costs for welding training. It's a $20,000 minimum," he protested.

"Marshall, generous people donate and corporations assist to help people like you."

"No one cares about me," he volleyed back. "Who would do that, anyway?" he continued. "Who would give that much money to help someone they don't even know?" His stubborn immaturity fought on.

"Marshall, there are a lot of caring, generous people out there who want to help you and people just like you," I said. "It's humbling to need their help. But sometimes, we need a helping hand," I continued. "One day, when you are on your feet, you can help others as you've been helped," I reassured him.

"Mom, I'm tired of leaning on other people," he mumbled. "It's embarrassing. Besides, that program can't be any good if it's only $150," he added.

"Give it a try, Marshall," I urged. "You have to be there by eight, and you can't be late!"

What he didn't know is I had gone there, met with the woman who would register him, and shared with her that he would enter looking like he had it all together but warning her of the thin thread holding him to this life.

A mother herself, she felt my panic, reassuring me she'd take good care of him. She did.

The next day, Marshall enrolled.

It was a two-month training program. That meant two more months with now, little income. A friend helped him land a part-time job with a cabinet company. He worked during the day and went to class at night. His bills piled up as he completed the course. Before graduation, I had arranged for him to shadow a man who owned a welding business. When he learned the social circle that working for David would expose him to, he was excited, yet intimidated.

"Wow, I'd be in *that* circle of people?" he asked. It involved Gina's young adult children and their families. This only added to the pressure and a greater fear of failure. Yet it spiked his enthusiasm, too. It was a double-edged sword for a kid in his fragile mental condition.

"Mom, I want to work for David, but I don't think he likes me," he said after meeting him. "The guys that work for him like me, though," he added, perhaps reassuring himself. "But the money isn't enough. I couldn't pay my monthly expenses much less all this debt."

I later learned David *did* like him, was impressed with him and interested in him, and I told Marshall so. But I didn't know how he'd make it financially, either. So we discussed the possibility of two jobs.

Standing on the edge of yet another cliff of opportunity and fulfilling a dream, Marshall was scared, immature, and impatient. He was right there at yet another breakthrough. He was just about to secure a job he'd actually enjoy, one in which he'd *feel* successful. He would have had a great mentor in David, too. Was he afraid he'd fail at this dream? The money, the disappointment, the pile-up of burdens overwhelmed him.

"Baby steps, Marshall," I'd say encouragingly. "How many times did I sit you kids down to tell you there was no financial way out? How many times did I show you the walls, ceiling, and floor of how boxed in we were? How many times did I say, 'This won't kill us, and when we are on the other side, it will be because of God?'" I fired those questions off in rapid succession.

"He will do the same for you. Just one day at a time. Sometimes it's one minute at a time," I continued.

But my words were beginning to fall on deaf ears.

"Arthur and I want to meet with you, Marshall," I continued.

He agreed. We met at the Mexican Inn for lunch. He wouldn't eat.

"I've already eaten," he said.

"Marshall, you have been traumatized. You can't keep stuffing your pain," Arthur counseled. "Remember when I drove you back to your old homes and you faced your father again for the first time after you left?"

He reminisced, sharing with Marshall the details of the scenario. "I never imagined a kid so afraid of his own father," Arthur continued. "You have been traumatized and need professional help getting to the bottom of this," Arthur added, pleading with him to accept professional help.

"We never went back after we left!" Marshall exploded. "That's a lie! How stupid! We would never have returned *there* after we left!"

"Marshall, I personally drove you back *there* twice," Arthur said in disbelief that he really didn't remember as it had only been four or five years since that time. "Yes, we all went back to help move furniture, get a few more items, and help prepare the homes to sell."

"That's stupid," Marshall insisted. "I don't remember any of this," he said tentatively, beginning to partially question himself.

"You don't remember? We emptied the attic in one house and moved things out of the garage of the other."

"I can't believe we would be dumb enough to go back. That's ridiculous," Marshall insisted.

Ridiculous. That's another one of his commonly used words. That, along with, Seriously?

"We had to go back to prepare the houses to sell. You have been so severely emotionally traumatized, Marshall, you blocked everything out," I explained. "Honey, you need to accept professional help. You have been traumatized and you have stuffed it way down deep. Please, let's get you help," I pleaded.

"Marshall, that day, I saw how traumatized and frightened you were. Get yourself some help. Please," begged Arthur, "listen to your mother."

"That's how traumatic facing your father was for you, Marshall," I added, keeping up the pressure. "You have suppressed your pain, stuffed it down so far into your 'tank,' you are about to erupt like a volcano inside.

"You need to accept professional help, Marshall," I continued. "The more you stuff down your pain and fear, the larger the monster grows. When you face it and call it what it is, you will realize it's but a little irritating bullying roach, a bottom feeder intent on creating more pain," I continued. "Your fear is harmless until you empower it, so face your fear, Marshall. Make friends with it."

If only he could see it was nothing more than something he could eventually flick off with a finger, stomp with a foot, and end, for good.

"Make *friends* with it?" He boldly stared me down. "Make friends with it? Are you kidding me? That's insane. No way!"

Mom, I need help, Marshall later texted.

Theresa at The Family Place lined up a counselor. Marshall and I went several times, alone, just us two. He eventually concluded that talking just didn't help.

I went to Marshall any time he'd text. I made suggestions. He shut them all down.

"I don't want the stigma of being a mental health patient. It stays on your record," he said, refusing help.

Having called suicide hotlines, hospitals, mental hospitals, a broad variety of programs, and anyone I could think of for help, I discovered no one would help me help him. That was because my son, at the age of 21, was considered an adult. He had to make the call himself. So I left Marshall with a list of numbers. Leaving him, I returned home, alone, to endure numerous sleepless nights of worry and prayer. He stopped answering my calls or responding to texts.

Sick with worry, I attended a women's inaugural event at The Fort Worth Club hoping to somehow soothe my soul. I asked to meet the man who created the "unveiled" logo, explaining to him that I speak and was writing a book about domestic violence.

"I don't know why I'm telling you this," he responded, "but I'm not supposed to be here." He explained how he had recently miraculously survived a suicide attempt, taking enough drugs to kill four men.

"I'll tell you why you are telling me," I said. "My son is home, and he's suicidal right now. Would you please go visit him?"

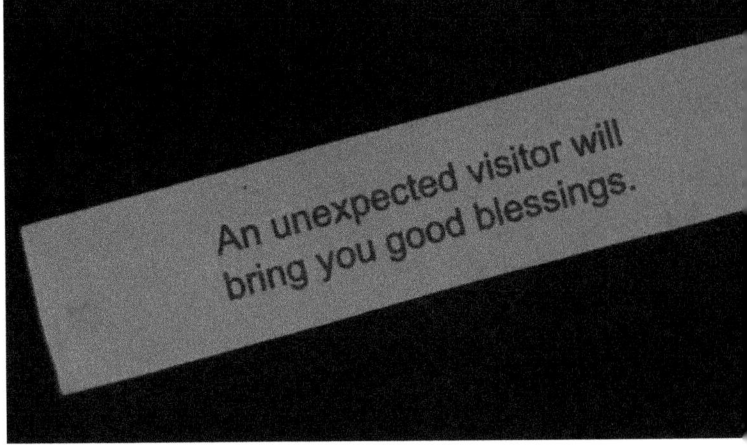

Found inside Marshall's locked box

"It's after nine in the evening," he said, looking at his watch. "Do you really want me to go now?"

After I described Marshall's situation, where he lived, and giving Barry Marshall's gate code and apartment number, he agreed to go.

"Are you going to tell him to expect me?"

"No, please just show up," I instructed. "He may or may not let you in."

Two hours later, Barry called.

"You've raised a fine young man," he said. "You should be very proud."

In pouring over all they discussed the past two hours, what stuck with me was Marshall saying to him, "I don't know if God is real."

To which Barry answered, "Son, you're not supposed to be here, you're a miracle. I'm not supposed to be here, I'm a miracle. You just opened your door to a stranger, a Black man you don't know, and we're sitting here on your couch discussing *God*?

"God sent me, son," Barry continued. "What more do you *need*?"

Barely holding on as if floating just beneath the water's surface, Marshall had three life rings floating nearby. *Swim to just one of them*, I'd pray. The life rings were not only Barry and David but also his true Ordinary Angel, Ever, the responding nurse in the emergency room at JPS hospital.

"Marshall. Please! Kick and swim, if just to one. Come up for air," I'd beg as he was sinking further from the surface away from me.

His eyes would lock on mine, telling me without words what he was already saying, *Mom, please let me go. You're the only reason I'm still here. Please understand.*

How this class influenced my life?

This class influenced me in many ways. For example, this class helped me learn more about Jesus. Not just about him but how to have a better relationship with Jesus. This class helped me noticed that being a Christian isn't a religion but it's a relationship. I always have had Jesus, God, the bible, and people shove everything about being a Christian down my throat. I used to believe that the only way to live right and get to be with Jesus in heaven was to do whatever people said Christians are supposed to be like. I used to always not want to be a Christian. Now, I feel more comfortable and confident with being a Christian now that I know that it's a relationship of love and not a forced religion. I'm happy I had this class because it truly changed part of my life. This class is a big part of my life testimony because it had a big impact on me. I am very thankful for my class mates and teachers. They all brought me closer to God than I have ever been. It's life changing.

-Marshall

June 1, 2011

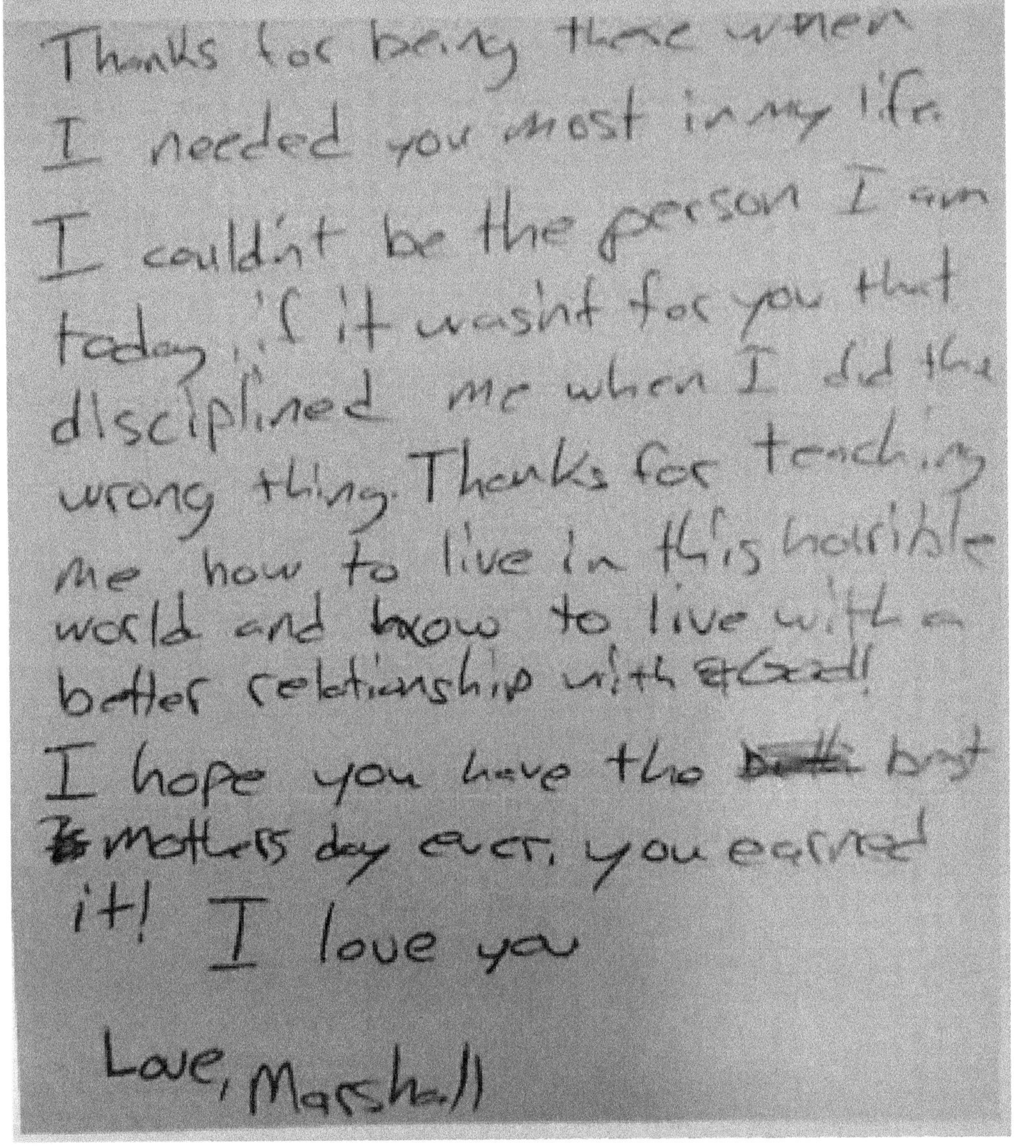
Thanks for being there when
I needed you most in my life
I couldn't be the person I am
today if it wasn't for you that
disciplined me when I did the
wrong thing. Thanks for teaching
me how to live in this horrible
world and how to live with a
better relationship with God!
I hope you have the best
mothers day ever, you earned
it! I love you

Love, Marshall

From the back of a Mother's Day Card. It reads,
Thanks for being there when I needed you most in my life. I couldn't be the person I am today if it wasn't for you that disciplined me when I did the wrong thing. Thanks for teaching me how to live in this horrible world and how to live with a better relationship with God!
I hope you have the best Mother's Day ever. You earned it! I love you.
Love, Marshall

"Hey mom, for my science research paper, I'm going to see if I can scientifically prove that God exists."
-Marshall (High School Sophomore Year)

I. Introduction

A. Is God Real?

B. If He is real, can we know Him?

II. Scientific Proof

A. Evolution

B. Creationism

III. Spiritual Proof

A. Answers in creation

B. Miracles documented

IV. Conclusion Does God Exist?

By: Marshall Foster

There are too many miracles in our universe to believe an explosion created the universe and all that is in it. There has to be a God to explain the universe and how it works together. And because of what Jesus said about himself being God in flesh, we must either believe him and follow him or believe he is a liar.

One miracle is that the earth size is perfect. If it was any bigger or smaller, it wouldn't be the right size to sustain life. If the earth was any closer to the sun it would burn up. If the Earth was farther away from the sun, the earth would freeze and all life would cease to exist. The moon is the perfect size also. And its distance is just right for its gravitational pull that creates ocean tides and movement to prevent water stagnation. This balance of gravity also keeps oceans from spilling over the land.

Water is another miracle. It is one of the substances no living thing can live without. Water keeps our body heat at a steady 98.6 degrees even in extreme temperatures. More than 95% of water is in the ocean. The system of evaporation is a miracle because this system cleans the salt of out the ocean water, lifts it into the cloud, the cloud floats over the land, rains on the land, filling lakes, feeding animals, plants, humans, and much more.

How is it possible that a jelly-like substance we call the "brain" can be responsible for our eyes being able to see color and objects, our bodies to feel temperatures, and feel your fingers touch. The brain can hold memories, thoughts, and emotions. The brain can function without you knowing. For example, breathing with your lungs which goes through your body and comes back and releases the old oxygen and your brain controls your heart beat without thinking about it and some people believe that the brain and everything else just popped out of nowhere (big bang theory) and evolved in to existence? More than a million messages are sent out by a human brain every second.

Each and every human cell has a DNA code with three billion letters to do different jobs. This also is a miracle. All computers act the same way as DNA code. Computers have numbers zero and one and the way they are arranged is the way they work just like DNA codes.

The laws of nature that never change suggest that an intelligent creator exists. The fact that our hot coffee will turn cold, the earth rotates in the same twenty-four hours, and the speed of light never changes. These laws cause the most atheistic scientists to call these mathematical mysteries "miracles."

Based on these findings I believe there is a God. For me, the "big bang" theory requires more faith. To believe in the big bang theory that all exists without any real purpose or hope for life beyond this life is harder to believe in that to believe in a God who created us and everything in and on this earth.

If God exists, then we must ask, "How did He get here?" If God is who he claims to be then he has always existed. He created everything. But how can we know God? Buddha, Muhammad, Confucius, and Moses said they all were prophets. Jesus is the only leader of any religion who said he was equal to God. Jesus preformed miracles. He made the lame to walk and the blind to see. Either he was God as he said he was and is the only way to

God as he said he was or he was a liar. I believe he was telling the truth. After he was crucified and his tomb was found empty, he was seen by 500 people. In our court system, it takes only one witness for them to believe something happened. Not one, but 500 people witnessed Jesus walking the earth after He had died. And then he disappeared.

If He is God, then I must learn what he says in the Bible and follow him according to his word. His claim of being God gives me no other option. "The heavens declare the glory of God; the skies proclaim the work of his hands." (Psalm 19:1) This is true. How the universe works proves God is real.

References:

Hppt://www.gotquestions.org/is-god-real.html

http://www.christain-faith.com/how-do-you-know-gods-real

http://www.christainanswers.net/q-aig/aig-c038.html

http://www.everystudent.com/feaures/is-there-a-god

In this paper, every OPINION from someone else has been acknowledged in a parenthetical citation. I realize that the mere presence of a parenthetical citation does not avoid plagiarism. If I have used the exact words, phrases, clauses, or sentences of someone else, I have enclosed that information in quotation marks. If I have summarized the opinions of someone else, I have not enclosed the summary in quotation marks; but I have stated those opinions in my own words. I have also introduced the summary and used a parenthetical citation to acknowledge the source.

ALL FACTUAL INFORMATION (common knowledge or uncontested knowledge), though not credited with a parenthetical citation, has been stated in my sentence structure. I have not used anyone else's organization of the factual information.

Signed: Marshall Foster

Barry's Story

I feel cheated. Twice has someone come into my life for me to share a very short time with, only to quickly lose them. First, it was my wife's grandfather, whom I met not long before he died. From our first moment together watching TV, he and I visited as if we had known each other for years. We lost him a few months later. I felt cheated.

Then it happened again when, just by chance, I was in the right place at the right time. As Susan Foster tells in her book, *Charming Impossibles: How Ordinary Angels Help Free the Hopelessly Stuck*, we met in October 2017 at a networking event. From our brief greeting, I ended up going to see her son, Marshall, for my first and, unfortunately, only time. But those few hours spent with him would be some of the most impactful few hours I'd ever spend with a "stranger." After hearing how very concerned Susan was for Marshall's mental health, being that neither she nor the family had really been able to get in face-to-face contact with him because of this episode of depression he was going through, I immediately went to Marshall's apartment to visit him. I had explained to Susan as we had talked that I had once tried to commit suicide and that my earnest attempt was unsuccessful, thanks to God.

Upon arriving, I knocked on Marshall's door, and it slowly opened to reveal a big man-child of a young man. I introduced myself and told him that I was a friend of his mom's and that she had asked me to come see him, since I knew something about how he was probably feeling because I myself dealt with depression. He said,

"Okay," and let me in. I had on a dark suit with an open-collared dress shirt and was afraid he might think I was some legal authority, yet he invited me in.

We first sat at his kitchen table. As I entered, I noticed the sofa to my left and a big screen TV by it that was turned on. The screen had a video game on it, but it was on pause with no action. I asked him if he had been playing. He answered, "Yes." It was definitely the apartment of a single young man. Not neat, but not messy. As I took my seat I kept thinking, This guy is not just tall, but big too! As big as he was, he was just that gentle. I told him that I had met his mom at an event at The Fort Worth Club earlier that night and that after the event, my wife, who knew his mom from various business events, introduced her to me. I let him know that I had designed a logo that was presented that evening for Platinum Women, a new group that was introduced during the event. I further explained that his mom wanted to talk to me about designing a logo for an organization she wanted to start about spousal abuse. I explained to him that while I did not experience spousal abuse, I did know firsthand about mental illness and that it oftentimes is connected to abuse. "That's when she told me about you," I explained to Marshall, hoping to connect for him why I was asked to come see about him, if he would talk to me. So there we sat. We talked about my past dealings with clinical depression that I had battled most of my life, that it ran through both sides of my family, and that it possibly runs through his, too.

I went on to explain that upon my being diagnosed in 1989, I was admitted to a mental health hospital through the employee assistance program at the company where I worked. I spent 20 days in the hospital going through the program and learning much about myself, past and present. I was put on my first antidepressant while in the hospital. I've been on antidepressants for over 30 years. I like to say, I'm as good at taking my antidepressant pill as women are at taking their birth control pill. I don't miss!

I shared my hospital stays and the success I had had with my stays and the doctors and my therapist. I asked Marshall questions about his past and his motorcycle that Susan had told me about during our brief encounter. As I watched him, I noticed he seemed comfortable with me, a complete stranger to him. I admired his curly hair to myself, thinking what a nice person he was. We talked about his past interactions with doctors and antidepressant medicines. I shared my history with him as it concerned those meds. I told him since I had been taking them, from the very first pill, the medication made me feel like "me." A me that I had never felt. I let him know it didn't make me feel high or drugged. The more I talked, the more I could see he wasn't in a "good" place mentally. We talked about the similarities in our fathers. There was physical trauma from my father when I was a kid and teen. After learning about my own father's childhood and family of origin, I understood him better because there was physical and mental trauma within his family when he was a kid. It doesn't excuse his actions, but it helped me learn and determine to never carry that behavior into my relationship with my son. After years of individual therapy, I discovered that not only did I have clinical depression, but through family work on my childhood, I discovered that a lot of my anger as a child came from the lack of serotonin in my brain. The lack of serotonin has also been linked to childhood trauma.[7]

Unfortunately, in the early 1960s when I was a child, mental illness was not something talked about in society. My doctors and therapist have theorized that, as a baby, I most likely suffered from separation anxiety. I had to be within eyesight of my mother as a baby. As I grew into a child, I had to know where my mother was at all times, and if she was away (like the time she and my dad went on a vacation to New York City when I was about eight years old), I would cry for days and most of my waking moments. Although I loved my dad, it was my mom to whom I seemed "addicted." Marshall and I discovered we both shared similar childhood anger issues and strong bonds to our mothers as well. My mother attempted suicide when I was 13. Thankfully, it was unsuccessful. She survived it and went on to live a very mentally healthy life until her passing. As a family, we discussed it openly from the time it happened and throughout our lives. Later, I would learn that Marshall's grandmother had attempted suicide. While both women were diagnosed with mental illness, with regard to their attempts, they also both were each responding to trauma they were enduring at that time in their lives. It's ironic, but some people may think that because I went through the traumatic suicide attempt as a kid with my mother, the chances of me trying it would be very slim. Well, though I understood firsthand the pain that a family suffers—even with just an attempt—my own depression was my own. I was in therapy. I was on my antidepressant, but my depression got so dark and deep, I just wanted the excruciating mental pain I was suffering from, the feelings and things I was going through, to just stop. Looking back, what I know is that I was back in my habit of isolating myself mentally and physically. But it's the mental isolation that is invisible, even to the closest people in your life. That's why when you know a loved one or a friend or acquaintance deals with depression, it's important to check on them often. Ask the question, "How's it going?" And don't "dig," but have a dialogue about how you'd like to simply check on them because you care about them. My family checks on me quite a bit. We talk openly about my mental state. It helps a great deal. I'm thankful that they do and I stay away from isolating my thoughts and moods. It's the greatest form of love that one can receive. We have to remove the stigma of mental illness and talk openly about it. Marshall was very concerned about the stigma. Marshall and I chatted about what he wanted to do with the rest of his life going forward. He was friendly but reserved.

Then, I decided to take our conversation to a place Susan told me that I may not want to go with Marshall—God. She said Marshall had struggled with his belief in God or whether there even was a God. I know that's not unusual when one is in a depressed state. You may wonder, If there is a God, why doesn't God stop this excruciating pain I feel?! I gave him my history and how I had been traumatized by a pillar of a woman in our Sunday school. She said to me, "Barry, if you don't get baptized you are going to hell!" That scared me beyond belief. I was about eight years old.

Marshall asked me questions and I gave him answers. I told him that I had tried committing suicide on June 3, 2016. I had taken enough subscription medicine to kill four people—124 pills! I told him that only God could arrange for me to be here still, on Earth, sitting and talking with him.

I had been in a coma for three days and my body began shutting down; the intensive care doctors asked my wife if I had a DNR—a do-not-resuscitate order. I did. They told my wife that my organs were shutting down and there wasn't anything more that they could do for me. Well, on the third day, God brought me out of the coma. I asked Marshall if he could see that by what I had been through with my suicide attempt, that there had to be a God. And the fact that what I read about the medicines indicated I took enough to kill three—maybe four—people, didn't kill me. Nor did I even suffer any physical ailment—which was considered likely from ingesting so much. When I think about the blessing I received from God as I know Him, in saving my life when the doctors said there was nothing more they could do for me, there's not a day that goes by that I don't thank Him. Many days I thank God numerous times a day for saving my life. Marshall and I spent a little over two hours together. During that time, he gave me his undivided attention. I asked him if he would he at least reach out to his mom or brother or sisters and get some help. He wouldn't commit to my request. I gave him my number and asked if he felt he was going to do something to himself, would he at least call me, so we could talk more? I told him my phone was on 24/7/365. I told him he could call me at any time and I'd be there. He wouldn't commit, but he took my number. I said to him that I had better go so I could call his mom and let her know we had talked, because I knew she was extremely worried about him. He said, "Okay." He walked me to the door and we shook hands. He said goodbye and I said see you later.

I had mixed feelings, but I hoped and prayed that I'd see Marshall again.

I went to the parking lot and sat in my car to call Susan. I told her I felt that, mentally and emotionally, he wasn't in a good place. That he definitely needed help from a doctor, that I tried to get him to commit to getting it. I wanted to give her my honest hope, but I knew I couldn't, unfortunately, promise anything. Susan thanked me and I told her to call me at any time, 24/7, and we said our goodbyes.

A few days later Susan called me and gave me the tragic news. My heart was broken. I knew that if mine was broken, Susan's and his brother and sisters' hearts were crushed beyond belief.

I felt that I had failed Susan and her kids. I talked to my wife and my brothers about my feelings of failure, but they encouraged me that I had tried, and some people wouldn't have had the courage to do what I did.

That one sit-down with Marshall Foster changed my life. Meeting with Marshall changed it in ways that, in this life, he never knew. His apartment complex was near the Fort Worth Costco. Every time I go to Costco, I think of my friend Marshall and the wonderful young man that his mom, Susan, allowed me to meet. Even for just a few hours. But once again, I feel cheated.

—Barry G. King

In 1975, at the age of 11, Barry won first place in a worldwide art contest sponsored by UNICEF for Children, which was entered by children from around the world. The King family had been friend to a certain young man named Cassius Clay in his formative years, growing up in Louisville; later, Barry's father, George N. King Sr., became Muhammad Ali's personal trainer. One of Barry's regular subjects, therefore, has been the world-famous boxer.

On October 16, 1975, Barry presented one of these drawings to Ali. He purchased it on the spot, and then surprised Barry by inscribing it with a special note and returning it to him. Ali had written that Barry would be a great artist on day. Barry's personal favorite of his Ali drawings is that of Al and his wife, Khalilah, with his mother, Miss Odessa, in 1976. The curator of the Ali Center in Louisville, Kentucky added a copy of Barry's original drawings of Ali to the center's permanent collection.

In 2005, Motown recording artist Marvin Gaye purchased Barry's original drawing, "The Five Faces of Marvin." Most recently, Barry's work has been displayed at The George W. Bush Presidential Library and Museum in Dallas, Texas.

You can find Barry's work at www.etsy.com/shop/PaintingWithAPencil.

One additional point of interest about Barry: Barry G. King played the office manager opposite Denzel Washington in the movie John Q.

PART 3

"I loved you your whole life. I'll miss you for the rest of mine."
– Parent of child in heaven

Like a numb manikin, I robotically smiled, shook hands, and hugged the guests at my 21-year-old son's funeral.

Marshall's struggle was over, but ours had kicked into even higher gear. There his body lay, the baby of four, in his favorite blue blazer, khaki pants, and tie, presented on a puff of white satin on display like a box of fine chocolates. I knew in that moment that shock is our body's gift to us. It protects us from feeling, temporarily anyway. Shock was fueling my every move those days.

My son took his own life. He was only 21. How do I digest this unwanted, rotten pill lodged in my throat? How do his three surviving siblings and I live on without him? These fleeting thoughts warranting a complete emotional breakdown were stifled with duties such as gathering photos; discussions about whom to be sure to inform; creating a program; picking the cast as if we were putting on an entertainment show; and choosing flowers . . . all leading to this evening before the final morning service.

With the planning complete, a funeral director takes over, keeping us following the order of events I faintly recalled even creating. Numb, denying myself the ability to feel, my three children and I enter the room dressed in gorgeous flower arrangements gifted from friends. Those arrangements frame the decorative box in which my son is displayed.

I walk over to kiss Marshall's forehead. It's cool to the touch of my lips. He's not there. It's not him.

It is his brown curly hair. It's the hair I cut for years with shears on the back porch. Holding a hand mirror, he'd instruct me: "Can you cut a little more here, Mom?" or "Not too much from there." Because of his hair's bristly nature, he didn't have many style options. Style was simply *shorter*.

It was the same hair his high school graduation cap adorned.

"We've just got to get this boy graduated," his principal would say every time I was called in for Marshall's angry outbursts. "He's a good kid," he'd say. "Marshall's just been through a lot," he'd say, revealing patient understanding.

I flashed back to all the meetings I had with coaches trying to get Marshall involved in sports. The broken arm from horsing around with friends one summer left him on football field sidelines, bored and discouraged. Learning disabilities kept him from making grades to compete in wrestling. Having rejected the ADHD medicines that temporarily helped him focus but left him with unwanted side effects, he'd find solutions in trying a different school. Each new high school year he wanted to try a new school. Four different high schools later, he finally graduated from a charter school. Not proud of himself as I was, he did it.

"I don't want anyone else coming to my graduation, Mom," Marshall insisted. "Only you," he said.

Sitting alone in the crowd, Marshall walked by looking right into my eyes with that half-crested smile I knew well. He was shyly saying, *I am kinda proud of myself, actually.*

"We can meet after his ceremony to celebrate at a restaurant," Aunt Gaye offered, providing a fantastic compromise. At the restaurant with family all around us, I hear, "Thanks, Mom. I am glad I went through the ceremony," as he gave me a memorable bear hug.

Touching his hair nestled up against white satin, I'm reminded it's also the same hair I caressed when finding him lifeless on his couch in his apartment with a gun in his hand at his side. The peace I saw on his face at that moment, I don't see now. He looks hollow. He doesn't look like how I found him after Winston and his friend kicked open the door. When I found him, he looked peacefully asleep on a red wet blanket.

Falling to my knees onto his big bear chest, I cried, "I love you!" in an agonizing deep guttural groan, a sound I'd never heard from myself before. "Oh my God, I love you,

Marshall," I repeated over and over, caressing his hair, kissing his face, holding him as my sleeve sopped up his blood.

Yes, let my sleeve sop up what's left of his life. I want it on me. I want him. I want whatever is left of my son. Let it touch me, get on me. It's his blood that my body gave him when he was in my womb. It's our blood. What came from him is on my sleeve now. I'll keep it. I'll keep it forever.

The police, who had patiently waited, interrupted my grief, saying, "You'll have to go now. This is a crime scene."

A crime scene, my son's death is a crime scene?

As an officer bent over me as I gave my son one final caress, I hear him say, "He did his research. He knew right where to aim."

That would be Marshall. He would do that to make it as tolerable as possible. And before the police ushered us out, Winston picked up a sheet of paper.

"Eviction notice," he read out loud.

It had been taped to his door the day before.

"That would have pushed me over the edge, too," he said, weeping. Marshall had torn up checks that I had given him to help with that.

As I stand over Marshall's coffin, I can't help but think how peaceful he looks. But I'm actually grateful to have seen him then so that the shallow remains I see in this satin-lined box is not my only memory.

As I touch his hands folded nicely over the blue blazer he proudly purchased for himself, memories flood my heart.

* * *

Modeling his then brand-new blazer in the mirror, Marshall looked at me in anguish. "I don't know how to tie a man's tie," he said dejectedly.

"Let's go to a men's dress shop together and have a sales associate teach you about men's clothing," I replied. The store manager not only gave him a lesson on dressing but also hired him part time in sales. Marshall worked through the holidays and, with his extra money, bought himself his first suit and this blue blazer.

"The other sales associates don't believe I really don't know the different types of collars," he shyly reported to me, suffering embarrassment after his first day. "That's why you are there, to learn," I reassured him. "Don't worry about what they think. I'm so proud you are working two jobs as you make money learning what you've been seeking to learn. It takes guts."

He finished out the holiday season with a really nice wardrobe and a new confidence. He knew how to dress, when to button and unbutton his jacket, and was really proud he bought his own suit.

"I bet most people think my parents bought me my suit," he shyly said, smiling

proudly one day while I watched him tie his tie. "I'm proud I bought this myself."

He worked hard at pushing himself forward. He had accomplished quite a lot. At 17, he was providing well for himself; had his own apartment, truck, and insurance; and a great start at AT&T as a cable technician.

* * *

Those are definitely his hands, I notice, caressing his hands folded so neatly together. They are the same hands (only bigger) that I held when he was a toddler fidgeting on my lap, wanting to run loose to run wild during his older brother's basketball game. They were the same hands I guided as he learned to tie his own shoes. They were the same hands that reached out to me to hold him when he was unsure about staying in the church nursery. They were the same hands that demonstrated the raw power of his motorcycle as he revved it up. They were the same hands that I held again in the hospital, a month later after his miraculous recovery. They were the hands I loved all his life that gave great, wonderful bear hugs. They were the hands I would forever miss.

People, oh yes, people are here for me to greet. As I turn through the crowd of mourners in black, I saw him enter, making his way to me, bypassing the open casket presenting the human shell that no longer held my youngest son.

How is it that here, at my son's funeral, this acquaintance coming toward me, whom I met only weeks prior, is now one of the most important people to me?

Sweat dripping down his tensed jaw, his eyes locked on mine, he forges through the crowd as if on a mission to stand boldly before me to confess, "I failed."

Pausing, bracing himself for my expected response, he waits. I slowly begin nodding my head, wincing to emphatically denounce his declaration.

"Oh no, Barry," I said. "You did not fail."

As tears began to fall, I continued through clenched teeth, holding my fist in the air, "You, Barry, are the sole reason this mother isn't shaking her fist at God asking Him, 'Why didn't you intervene on behalf of my son?!'"

With tears streaming my cheeks, I tried to ease Barry's misplaced shame and guilt.

"Barry," I said, "you were right when you told Marshall that God sent you to him. I thought God sent you for my son, but He sent you to my son *for* me."

No one could possibly know the thin shredding thread tethering my faith. My hope hung, barely attached, but, yes, attached, because of Barry's conversation with Marshall the last week of his life. In a moment, Barry transformed from a complete stranger to a deep, reliable confidante, a friend of my soul.

And I'd known him all but one week.

Relaxing his jaw, taking deep, shaky breaths, he receives my message. It obviously resonates with his truth. He knew he wasn't guilty, but he wanted to be prepared should I have considered him so.

Our encounter was bigger than all three of us. It was as if we were part of scripted play. Like genius actors going off script in a production, we observed as we participated. With the star of our three-cast show gone, his remains lying in a box soon to be closed forever, Barry and I agree to later revisit what the original intent and purpose for our meeting was that fateful evening.

Barry left in peace.

* * *

Throughout the days and grief-filled nights following Marshall's passing, I read through Marshall's text messages. I read over and over again our messages to one another, looked at the timing, and what was going on when this was said or that happened. Finding photos of his high school girlfriend, I contacted her. From her I learned that she had moved five hours away, inviting Marshall to join her when they graduated from high school. He thought about it, she said, but ultimately decided against it.

Asking Sophia if she knew of this, she responded, "Yes, he thought about it but believed it would be best for her if he let her go rather than expose her to all our drama."

Looking over Marshall's big smile with happy eyes in every photo he took with his girlfriend, I grieved. She sent me a photo of a painting he created of the two of them walking a moonlit beach with footprints in the sand. I sobbed, accepting yet more loss. She showed me photos of birthday roses he had given her with a card reading, "Will you accept this rose?" He loved her so.

Marshall painted this for his girlfriend when they were in the 9th grade. It still hangs on her wall.

Dear Mrs. Sexton,

My name is Marshall Foster. I recently moved to Arlington at the end of my eighth grade year. I came from a town called New Braunfels. We moved because my mother and father divorced.

What makes my life most interesting for me is my girlfriend. She has been a true friend for me and has helped me during this tough time. I played football and was a starting defensive tackle on a 5A, A-team. But, then I broke my hand and was out all last season. This season I am out because of my back. Now I am in strength and conditioning and hope to get stronger so I can play again.

What I really like best about school is my French class. I have been very excited to learn French and I can't wait to see what I can do with it after high school. I'm hoping to go study abroad in France during college. And maybe I will discover or find a way to get a job where I can use my French language skills. This will be very exciting to me.

Finally, I hope you will be glad I am in your English class because I hope to do very well. And I'm trying to make this a good year for myself. Most importantly, I hope to keep up my grade average.

Sincerely,

Marshall Foster

But due to the psychological warfare and abuse of a Charming Impossible, my son chose to protect the love of his life from his father by rejecting the love he needed, deserved, and that she longed to offer. She was his Ordinary Angel, but he didn't understand that. Ordinary Angels are equipped to walk beside us. We may not like feeling vulnerable, allowing them to see our pain and suffer along with us, but that's part of their journey. To deny an Ordinary Angel their purpose robs them, too. I hope others learn from Marshall's mistake. He should have allowed her in, open himself wide, and let God use her and grow her as she helped him heal.

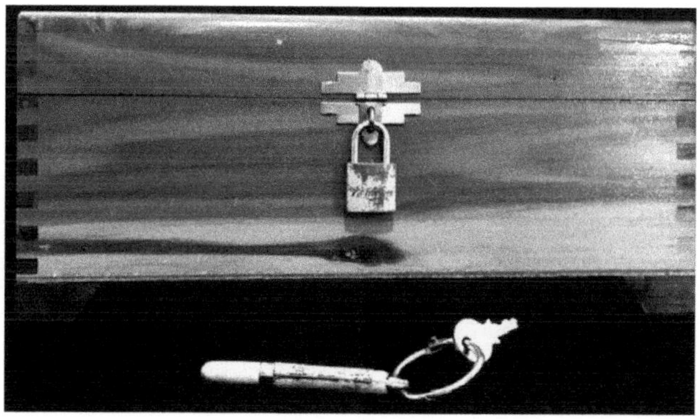

The locked box

All Marshall's friends and siblings knew of—and were curious about—a box Marshall kept locked away from everyone. It was secret, a special treasure of Marshall's that was off limits, and no one could get near it. Marshall was extremely private, and his most sensitive belongings were locked inside that box. He was so protective over it, it became a joke among the gang. It was no joke to Marshall: He made it clear that they were never to open it, nor should they ever make the attempt.

After his passing, Sophia grabbed the box. Alone, she opened it to find a box, locked inside a box, locked inside a chest that had Kaitlin's cheerleader picture, her love letters, and memorabilia from time they spent together. Sophia also found Audrey's modeling agency photo card and fortune cookie messages of hope and a future tucked inside. In fact, some of Marshall's writings in this book, which are presented in their original, unedited form, were also found inside.

That Marshall pushed away love because of all our family drama broke my heart. Emotional abuser's tentacles are so far-reaching. If only they would let their Targets go when they leave, allowing them space to heal.

Unfortunately, they don't. Like killer bees, they keep stinging until their victim is down . . . and then they eat them from the inside out.

Scrolling through Marshall's phone text messages became more and more a way to feel close to him. No longer was I seeking answers or peace of mind about "what ifs." It was rather my way to hear his voice. That's when I came across an almost year-old message Marshall had had with Ever, the responding nurse from the emergency room at JPS. Ever was also a motorcyclist. He was with Marshall when Marshall was brought in by ambulance directly following his wreck. They had an immediate connection even before Marshall's miraculous, life-saving surgery. The thought of this man took me back to that day.

From the texts I gathered that Ever had connected with Marshall following his discharge from the hospital. Ever evidently met with Marshall offering to help him sell the cycle for parts or repair it, if possible. Then Marshall suddenly stopped responding.

The final business left for me with what Marshall left behind was this motorcycle. I didn't know what to do with it. My friends in the car business were not interested and didn't know anyone who was. His cycle was in a storage unit with the rent due.

Needing to find it a home, I texted Ever: *I don't know if you remember me, I'm Marshall's mother. I need to do something with Marshall's wrecked cycle. Would you be interested in it for parts?*

Coming straight from work, still in his blue scrubs, Ever met me at the storage unit. When I handed him Marshall's key, Ever unlocked the lock and slid open the metal door. There sat Marshall's "baby" . . . his pride, his shattered dream. Seeing Marshall's shattered dream, I wept. I fell into that deep, dark place of unrestrained pain, loss, and despair.

The last time I had been to this storage unit was the day Marshall was discharged from rehab. I had just loaded his wheelchair into my trunk and folded him into the front seat with his arm in a cast and his leg in a brace.

"Mom, please take me to see my motorcycle."

That was his first request.

Sliding open that metal door of his storage unit, Marshall hoisted himself from his wheelchair, hopping on one foot, to embrace his bike in a desperate plea, "Why, why, why . . .?" was all he could say, draping himself over his bike, hugging it.

I wondered the same damn thing. *Why? Why can't you give this kid a break? Seriously!* I yelled out silently to God as if this was all God's fault! *Of course, I'm grateful you saved his life. I'm grateful you placed him with the best doctors and staff.*

I continued my quiet conversation with God while Marshall mourned his own loss.

Yes, it's amazing Marshall said he was falling in front of the semi on the highway when he felt a force gently catch him and push him into the grassy median. Yes, it's amazing the policeman happened to be driving by just after Marshall and his cycle rolled, flew through the air, and landed on the median. Of course, it's miraculous he didn't sustain spinal or otherwise debilitating injuries considering the ridiculous speed we know Marshall was going due to his GoPro attached to his bike. I know all the unexplained miracles for his body! I know! But what about his heart and his will to live? How do I encourage him now? I silently demanded. *I'm scared!*

Months later, there I stood again, this time with Ever in Marshall's stead. Ever looked over the bike, patting it like it was an old friend. We both stood looking, staring, just being for the moment. Then Ever reached up, grabbing the handle to lower the sliding door. He locked the unit with Marshall's

Ever, Susan and Barry at the MRP33 "Reveal."

lock, tucking Marshall's key in the top pocket of his scrubs.

"I have something for you," he said.

Handing me a wrapped gift, he added, "It's from my wife and me. I have an uncle who committed suicide."

When I unwrapped the gift, I found a devotional and card with a beautifully handwritten note of condolence from Ever's wife.

Pointing across from Marshall's unit, he said, "See that unit just two doors down? That's where my bike is stored. I learned about this storage unit from Marshall."

Marshall's bike was an old friend of his, after all. It was more fitting that Ever have Marshall's bike than I realized. Seeing Ever in his scrubs took me back to when Ever would visit Marshall post-op in his hospital room.

* * *

"I bought you something, Marshall," Ever said, handing him a metal hand on a stick. "It extends, see?" demonstrating how Marshall could use it to grab things or to scratch when he had an itch inside of his cast.

"Thank you," Marshall said, cracking a rare smile. It was a moment of unasked for kindness . . . thoughtful, caring, and above and beyond, nice. A moment so crucial that I have the memory of Marshall's then oh-so-rare smile ingrained in my heart forever. Ever would stop by and sit with Marshall, just because. And now, I'm handing over my son's dream, his everything to Ever. And I'm so grateful someone properly fitting is available to receive it.

Months later, Ever asked to meet with me and the hospital director of trauma, Mary Ann. He had a surprise, something very special, he said, and wanted us to be there for the presentation.

Ever was a nurse, not an event planner, so as he tried to explain to Mary Ann and me about how he'd like to make this presentation, we looked askance at one another trying to understand what he had in mind. Not really sure what to expect, Mary Ann and I agreed to come, inviting a few others.

"So, what is this, again?" I heard from certain friends and invitees.

"I honestly don't know," I said. "This is a nurse putting on an event for our family, but he can't really tell us about it because he wants it to be a surprise. If you want to come, here's the address."

Ever did share that he created a website titled MRP33. It stood for "Marshall Racing Project 33." With what little information he shared, I could tell Ever was putting a great deal of effort in this. I decided to create a t-shirt for those who attended to show support for Ever. With my event planning background, I sensed Ever had a vision for how this should or could go. By the time of the event, we had over 30 people show up to a racetrack on the outskirts of town. None of us had ever been there.

Ever, Susan, and Barry at the MRP33 "reveal"

Barry came. I loved seeing Barry in the green t-shirt. We were brought into a crowded room of 100 plus Ninja "crotch rocket" racers.

This is a statue of what it feels like to be a parent who has lost a child.

"Okay, everybody, listen up!" The leader of group took charge.

"We have a special presentation today, but before we get to that, we have some business to cover."

The leader of the pack went over the regular "drill."

"Safety first," he said, explaining that this was not a race against others but against themselves. He encouraged the seasoned riders to not hesitate to tell a less experienced rider to ease up if they were pushing beyond their experience or training. He led and taught this group of men how to mentor and willingly be mentored. He closed with a prayer asking for safety for all riders.

So this is where Marshall was meant to land. With mentors and "safety first." Ever tried to introduce this to Marshall, bring him into this fold. Had Marshall not had his wreck, he never would have met Ever. This would have been a dream come true for Marshall.

Ever's Story

Marshall came into my life as a trauma patient. In the trauma unit, I remember we were alerted over a paging system that a trauma patient was coming. We were discussing his case while he was en route by ambulance. While we were all prepping and being prepared to receive him, we were told it was a motorcycle wreck. Right after his surgery, Marshall was assigned to me. He landed in my hands.

Almost immediately after meeting him, within an hour or so, I knew something was different about him. He kept guarding himself. I wondered, Why is he so seemingly detached from what he's experiencing? The way he should be behaving after this kind of trauma should be very different. And when we do assessments, we expect certain typical answers. His answers were anything but typical.

I would expect a normal kid in pain to ask for pain medicine, to verbalize typical answers to the questions we ask about pain. Most trauma patients are pretty verbal about what they are going through. Marshall was very . . . "I'm doing okay."

I'd ask, "Do you need pain medicine?"

"I'm okay," he'd reply.

"Marshall, Can I do anything for you?" I'd dig deeper.

"I'm okay. I'm doing great," Marshall would insist, smiling really big.

A person who is broken into a bunch of pieces with a missing spleen should not be smiling a lot. Whenever I would come into his room, he would have episodes of smiles, acting like he was doing great, but when I would close the door and peek through the window (when he could not see me,) I could see he was in great pain. I could tell he was toughing it out to the maximum. What he was saying was not correlating with what I was seeing. I was not seeing or hearing what I should be from a trauma patient.

Eventually, I gave him some pain medicine and encouraged him to take it. "You need to take this medicine, Marshall."

He did.

Now, a lot of patients are not that compliant. Marshall was one of these rare individuals who followed what he was ordered to do.

When he hit the call button, he'd always apologize. I'd say, "I'm doing my job. Me helping you is doing my job."

Still, every time he hit the call button, he would apologize: "Hey, I'm sorry to bother you but. . . ." I had to keep reassuring him, "We are here to help you. . . ." And things like that. I picked up that something with him wasn't right.

I met two of his siblings who came to be with Marshall and was told his mother was en route. Marshall's older sister and brother were very supportive of him, well mannered, friendly, and most importantly, they gave Marshall his space. It was clear they were there for him, but they never interfered with his care or medical decisions.

Immediately feeling a connection to Marshall, I observed he had such a . . . I don't want to say naïve, but rather a good nature of no malice. It became clearer to me that Marshall perhaps didn't have the perspective of "This is not normal, this is not right."

A shattered arm, a broken leg, and a missing spleen is not normal. But he responded as though he was expected to act like it was. Asking for pain medicine is not bad. But he didn't seem to know that. I was assigned to him three days to take care of him as a bedside RN and then I was team-leading on that floor in a supervisor role. Marshall and I connected on being riders. We both had the very same motorcycle at the time. Through our growing connection, I observed that he seemed to struggle with what evil looks like in the world, as if he didn't seem to know how to do harm. He didn't really understand it.

When Marshall moved out of the ICU, I continued to check on him and was determined to keep an eye on him throughout his stay. By the time Marshall's mother, Susan, came in, Marshall had left the trauma unit and was moved to another floor. I came to meet her when she arrived. Pulling her aside to tell of my observations about Marshall, I explained that he seemed ethereal, innocent, and not responding as a usual trauma patient would.

After Susan explained there was abuse in their background, it all began to make sense to me; due to the trauma Marshall went through as a child at home, he was led to believe he was supposed to put up with that trauma, that he was to "tough it out."

As a nurse, I had to maintain a professional boundary. I did not want to get too emotionally attached to Marshall. I treat my patients nicely—like my own family—without getting too attached, because anything can happen. Sometimes, we do get attached to our patients whether we like it or not. It's part of nursing. It happened to me the moment I met Marshall. It did happen. I did get attached to him . . . and here I am.

One day while in the hospital gift shop, I noticed a metal extendable-hand back scratcher and immediately thought of Marshall; during my prior visit with him, I saw him scratching an itch using a pen down the cast on his arm. He then grabbed a fork as he was struggling to scratch an itch on his back.

Picking up the scratcher, I kind of laughed. Looking at the extendable hand, I was thinking, Marshall might like this This has Marshall's name all over it. This will be Marshall's scratcher. Then, I looked at it again and thought, this is dumb, and put it back. That's when I started second-guessing myself: Should I give it to him? I kept second-guessing myself wondering, Is this stupid?

I bought it anyway.

At home that evening, I showed the scratcher to my wife, Enny. By then, Enny knew all about Marshall. In fact, my whole racing team knew about him. I found myself talking about him, which was very unusual. I rarely talked about my patients on a personal level. With Marshall, it was different. It was so different that I was even emotionally preparing my team to meet Marshall.

As a team of high-speed racers, this riding team operates a bit on the cliquish side, meaning we don't let just anyone join us. We are a team: We travel together, race together, and get along well. With just a slight motion, we comprehend each other, understand what each other is saying, and have our own language while riding. It's a "special zone." So to bring someone into that zone (or group), the group gets prepped. "Hey, there's this person I want to invite in. . ." letting them know that somebody else is coming. That is why I told these guys about Marshall.

Knowing about Marshall's wrecked bike, Eli was willing to buy the bike for parts because he had a wrecking yard. Ruben is a mechanic and was looking forward to helping Marshall rebuild the bike. He owns RPM Ruben Perez Motor Works. Ruben even said, "Bring him to the track, that way he learns the track." I invited Marshall to the track while he was still in the hospital.

Racing requires being able to read each other's body language, learning how to anticipate the next move. Racing at such high speeds, we must be selective who we invite "in," for safety reasons as well as social. I believed Marshall would fit in well with us. My team was looking forward to meeting him. I was hoping to introduce this kid, Marshall, into the fold after his hospital discharge.

Before I finished telling Enny about the scratcher, I tossed it onto a shelf, talking myself out of giving it to him, feeling embarrassed to have mentioned it. Enny encouraged me to give him the gift. She encouraged me to follow my initial impulse.

Marshall loved it. Susan was there when I came in with it. It was a big hit.

While Marshall was no longer my patient, I kept checking in on him and his progress. His X-rays were pretty gnarly. His arm was broken in so many places, he received the longest metal bar ever to bolt together a forearm. The orthopedic team was left with one final surgery decision. Do they repair his leg now or later? Due to the fragile nature of the procedure, Marshall would be required to stay off his leg an entire month. The medical team discussed whether a 21-year-old young man would commit to remaining completely "no loadbearing" an entire month. I went to Marshall, explained the necessity of this procedure, the gravity of not following orders, and was able to convince the team to trust in Marshall so that he could put all the surgeries behind him and get back to the life he had awaiting him.

A month later, when Marshall returned for his final medical review, the entire orthopedic team who worked on him was there to greet him and assess whether his leg surgery was a success. After Marshall and his mom walked out of his appointment, even they could hear the team cheering behind closed doors. They were all so proud and happy for Marshall and for the shared medical success.

Following his hospital discharge and after Marshall started back to work, I met him at the storage unit. We followed each other to the unit containing his bike. By now, I'd bought a new bike and had lots of parts from my old bike that would fit on Marshall's. I had texted Marshall that he could have the parts for $5. (This was one of the texts Susan would later read.) Once again, I invited him to come out to the track sometime. We again discussed selling his bike versus the cost to rebuild it. The last thing that I got from him was that he did want to fix his bike. He did not want to give it up. I reassured him it was doable and told him one member of my team was a mechanic and another had a junk yard, a great resource for parts. I let him know that we all would be glad to help him. After learning of where Marshall stored his bike, I rented my own storage unit right across from him.

I never heard from him again.

One late night months later, I received a text message from Marshall's mother offering me Marshall's bike for parts. I called her first thing the next morning to hear what I feared—that Marshall had ended his life. This news landed me on the couch, and I wept.

With Marshall's bike in my custody, I considered selling it for parts or rebuilding it. A gnawing feeling that I needed to do something with Marshall's bike kept me considering my options. I feel like there is more to this bike, I thought continually. But what?

"I cannot bring Marshall back to life, but I can bring his bike back to life for Susan and the kids," I told Enny.

In the midst of putting Marshall's bike together, I began to think that it had a bigger meaning behind it. Many cultures are not good at talking about mental health. I had somewhat buried an incident that happened within my own family and had moved on from it. Or so I thought. But having lived through what happened to Marshall, I thought about the memory of my uncle who committed suicide, which is where I drew a line.

While working on Marshall's bike, I was reminded of the day I received a call from my cousin informing me that my mother's brother had committed suicide. The cousin could not bear to call my mom and asked me to make that call to her. My dad answered the phone that day and instinctively knew from my voice, because this uncle had called everyone that morning; we realized later that he was telling us goodbye.

"Is it your uncle?" my dad asked.

"Yes" was all I had to say.

Overhearing the conversation, my mother screamed in a wail of grief I will never forget. Then my mother came to the phone and I told her what I had heard from my cousin.

When my uncle had called my mother earlier that day, he said to her, "I'm done." He kept repeating he was done, that he was at peace, and that was it. When he called me, he seemed normal, and I could not pick up on what he was doing. He was well trained in the military at disguising his emotions.

With this surge of memories, I began to think, Why not do something more meaningful with this bike? And perhaps this will be a way suicide will not happen to someone else. Why not ride and talk about this?

I talked to Ruben, Dave, and Eli about my vision, my idea. I even shared with my superior at work what I was thinking about doing with Marshall's bike. She was wise and I respected her opinion. She encouraged me to do it. Her reassurance helped me move forward with this idea.

I had no idea how far this would go. I mainly wanted to do something for Susan and the kids to showcase Marshall's bike around the track. My idea was that everywhere I went, I'd have Marshall's bike around and people could ask about it. They might say, "That's a cool paint job, oh wait a minute, I see the name and dates," inspiring a conversation. My thought was that the bike would be a conversation starter about suicide and mental health.

Then the dark cloud of self-doubt set in . . .

Should I do this? I began to wonder. What will people think? It won't be well-received, I began convincing myself.

Fear. Fear of failure and of not being well-received created debilitating self-doubt that overshadowed why I was even attempting to do this.

My fear of failure was deeply rooted from my youth as my family immigrated to the United States from Cuba when I was 14 years old. Immigrating into a foreign country was traumatizing. Not speaking the language added excessive trauma. But we were grateful and excited to be here, where we would be given an opportunity with the hope to build for ourselves a way of life that we could keep.

In Cuba, my father was a farmer. We lived out in the country. We had land, cattle, and horses. We did not have running water or electricity. My father was very successful at what he did.

In Cuba, when he began making "too much" money, the government would come in and take half of our land. That's the way socialism works. My father paid hard-earned money to purchase land and a home for our family. He spent more hard-earned money keeping it well maintained and fruitful, owning it free and clear with no debt, only to wake up one day and have it taken from him because he had grown "too successful." This happens continually there. The government takes land, cattle, whatever they want, even if it's fully paid for, not with borrowed money, but with hard-earned sweat, work, and money. The Cuban government made it impossible for common people to get ahead.

Upon arrival to Miami, Florida, my father was offered the opportunity to participate in the American welfare system. I am grateful for my father's example in refusing it, requesting a job instead. At 14 years of age, I went from freely roaming the countryside on horseback, lavished in the love of friends, family, and plenty of food, to all alone in inner-city poverty, knowing no one. At school, the kids teased me because my Spanish sounded different from theirs. I didn't fit in with any group and quickly learned survival-of-the-fittest skills. It was dog-eat-dog. I had to become mean and tough or get devoured. By the time I turned 16, I was angry and even suicidal. It was the loving nurturing of my parents that held my feet to the ground throughout those years.

It was during these early years that I developed a need to prove myself, not only to myself but also to others. After experiencing betrayal and false "friendships" that were actually backstabbing in nature, I decided not to care about anyone but me. I didn't trust anyone, nor was I going to put myself in a position where I needed anyone. I would take care of me by myself. And I did. I learned that in the United States, anyone can make it, but not without a lot of hard work. So I worked extra hard.

When I learned that Marshall fled his own father, friends, and the life he knew at the age of 14, I better understood him. He, too, had developed trust issues and a desire not to ever need anyone. He developed the same "if it's to be, it's up to me" spirit that I had developed. Later, I would learn that Marshall had a "liar until proven honest" mentality, along with an "if I give you the chance, you'll take advantage of me" complex. He rarely trusted anyone, especially if they offered to "help" him. That was his sign they were "after" something he had, because he didn't truly believe anyone really cared about him. Other than his mother and a few others, he didn't believe it. That's the unfortunate truth about children of emotional abuse, they don't hate their abuser, they hate themselves and, therefore, engage in self-sabotage.

With my cycle of self-doubt and fear of failure raising its ugly head once more, Enny knew just what to say.

"If you have a burning idea that you keep coming back to, maybe you should just do it. If it's a flop, you did your part," she said.

After questioning myself and confirming why I was doing this, I came back to my first reason: This is for Susan and her family. I felt that having something of Marshall's that is still alive—that they can touch, see, and hear—would be a comfort.

It was during this wrestling within that I received a text message from Susan inviting me to meet at Starbucks. I met Susan and Marshall's brother that day, at which time Susan privately shared the video of their family that included Marshall speaking out about abuse and her coming book, *Charming Impossibles.* I returned to Enny from that meeting with a solid decision. Marshall is still with us through his bike. I would complete it and showcase it so as to start conversations.

And this is exactly what has happened. Marshall's bike is with us at every race. When people ask, we talk about it. People have thanked me for sharing about the bike and mental health awareness at the track and on Facebook. Many have said that they struggle with depression, and when they feel really dark, they go for a motorcycle ride. Riding is how they cope. It helps them to know they are not alone. People continually reach out, saying all this helps.

Only weeks following our meeting at Starbucks, during our family Thanksgiving gathering, Enny and I shared that Foster family video with Enny's parents, at which time they informed us of a newly discovered victim of abuse in their own family. As always, in giving or doing for others, we also receive. That Starbucks meeting had many unexpected results. The video Susan shared about abuse opened the eyes of my wife's family to abuse that was hiding in plain sight. The video helped us recognize our own blindness to a loved one suffering abuse right before our eyes.

Enny's family member was going through the same thing with her husband as Susan. The video had a strong influence on our recognizing that we had misjudged the victim for the abuser, a common misconception in these situations. Through Susan sharing her dilemma with us, we better understood what we were seeing in our own family situation and became better equipped to support her.

Since the publication of *Charming Impossibles*, many of our family members have read Susan's book, are better educated, and equipped with language to more fully discuss and understand the confusing web we all observed and misunderstood these past 10 years. Enny's family member no longer has to try to explain herself to family or close friends. She simply refers them to the book and says, "Yep, same story. . . ."

Another unexpected nugget was receiving the web link of Susan on the Jeff Crilley Show, sharing about the Marshall Racing Project 33. We sent this video to Enny's father, who is part of our church leadership. He presented the Jeff Crilley Show excerpt to the church leadership team, imploring them to recognize that when suicide happens in the church congregation, and the church falls short on talking about it, to consider how they, as a church, can better respond to the subject of suicide.

Meeting Marshall has changed my life. I want to be more like Marshall, in that he had a deep concern and love for others. As Enny will attest, I have often been very much about myself. She will also say, that after having met Marshall, I have become much more about others.

—Ever Gomez

Ever Gomez, a Practice Manager at John Peter Smith Health Network Pain Management Clinic, partners with the Medical Director and Community Health executives, to grow and develop a multimodal pain management approach to meet the needs of the community served. Within his first five years as a Critical Care nurse, Ever broadened his leadership career into serving as a RN Team Leader, ICU Manager, and Senior Clinical Director. Ever's expertise in excellent patient care is driven by building meaningful relationships involving bridges of swift communication and understanding between multidisciplinary healthcare teams and the patients they serve.

MARSHALL RACING
PROJECT 33

Ever is a Registered Nurse in the State of Texas, with diversified healthcare background. He has been recognized academically and professionally in the past with the Outstanding Achievement Award, Excellence in Clinical Nursing Award, and DAISY Award for Extraordinary Nurses.

Ever holds a Bachelors of Science in Nursing Degree from the University of Texas at Arlington.

In addition, Ever is the owner and founder of The Marshall Racing Project 33, a company dedicated to empowering individuals to talk openly about mental health issues in efforts to eradicate the silence and stigma associated with suicide, and to shine a light on suicide prevention by partnering with local resources to promote a community that is healthy and safe.

Many evenings and weekends were spent with Ruben, Dave, and Eli working on what ultimately would become The Marshall Racing Project 33, as we created from a totaled motorcycle a conversation starter for suicide and depression awareness. This dream couldn't have become a reality without the ongoing support of my wife and my friends, to whom I will forever be thankful and blessed to have in my life.

May Marshall's spirit continue to ride on with us!

www.mrp33.org

* * *

My heart sank at the loss of seeing the joy he would have experienced there. There, he would have had the many male mentors he often wished and longed for. There, he would have lived out his dreams with other like-minded men fulfilling their need for adrenaline in a safe, supportive environment. Marshall would have connected with these guys. He would have been at home there.

The general meeting came to a close. Ever stood, inviting me to the front of the room as he shared about meeting Marshall, who Marshall was to him, and how it came about that I had given him Marshall's motorcycle.

At the front of the room was a motorcycle covered by a sheet. Ever unveiled Marshall's motorcycle, and I fell onto it hugging it, weeping in disbelief and awe. It was painted green, Marshall's favorite color, numbered 33 for Marshall's birthday, March 3. Marshall's name was all over the bike. JPS and mental health awareness logos were beautifully displayed. It was a work of art. It was over-the-top gorgeous!

"I will race Marshall's bike for mental health awareness," Ever announced. "If you or someone you know struggles, come to me. Reach out. You are not alone."

Then Ever handed me a check made out to The John Marshall Foster Memorial Fund, a fund Dr. Haynes arranged after Marshall passed. Their generous donation to JPS, in Marshall's memory, goes to research on the effects of trauma to the brain.

* * *

Sunshine, wind, and fresh Texas spring air was the perfect backdrop for Marshall's bike debut. The crowd, resplendent in their green t-shirts, lined the track and the stands, cheering as Ever drove Marshall's bike around the track at rocket speed. Following the race, a professional photographer took photos of all of us with Marshall's bike and Ever. It was a day of awe. I marveled at who chose to show up. The event is where I met, for the first time, a high school friend of Marshall's. I met the parents of one of Marshall's friends there, too. It also brought Barry and Ever together for the first time.

One friend said that the event was life changing, unlike anything she'd ever attended. She said it was like everything surrounding Marshall's memory was organic, connected, without anyone running it. It was like a live movement without any one person in charge.

It was a beautiful, meaningful way for Marshall's memory to live on.

May he continue to touch people's lives, and may this movement prevent others from making the mistake he made. I only hope his life story encourages those struggling with depression to get the help they need. Through research we are learning how childhood trauma, emotional trauma, and physical trauma affect the brain. The John Marshall Memorial Fund at JPS established by Dr. Jay Haynes will continue to help fund this research and awareness. We are discovering new technologies and methods of healing for the brain every day.

* * *

Months following Ever's event, I sat back to absorb how Marshall's life is still impacting us and so many others. This brought comfort but didn't alleviate my struggle of feeling distanced from him. No Scripture, sermon, or affirming words of friends, family, or faith helped me find that peace of mind that Marshall was okay. The despairing cloud hovered over me. *Will this looming dark sadness ever go away? Did his sadness and struggle become mine?* I couldn't see a way out from under it. If only I could crawl in that grave with him became my companion-like thought. After all, a mother isn't supposed to outlive her child. I had lost loved ones. And it hurt. But losing a child is a sorrow all its own. It was a sorrow I wasn't sure I'd survive.

One day, Mary Ann from JPS called, asking to meet with me. In response to losing Marshall, Dr. Ghandi, the doctor who saved Marshall, the one Dr. Haynes lauded for performing the medical miracle that spared Marshall's life, began what he and the hospital chaplain named "The Trauma Circle."

"Let's invite the mother of that young man," he had said to Mary Ann during a planning meeting. This led to my finally getting to meet Dr. Ghandi.

"I'm Marshall's mother," I told him. "You saved my son's life. You gave me an extra year with my son. I've been looking forward to thanking you! Thank you!"

We were quickly seated in a circle of medical professionals discussing their own trauma.

"We don't even know the questions to ask with regard to trauma," admitted Dr. Ghandi. "I thought who better to start with than us, since we face trauma daily."

Marshall's story had led to the creation of this circle. After I shared my thoughts, Dr. Ghandi said, "I rarely meet my patients or their families. In fact, I usually don't even know the name of the person I'm operating on," he said. "Hearing the aftermath and effects on your family is doing something for me right now that I can't explain."

He doesn't get to see or experience the beautiful results of his work? I couldn't imagine working in trauma, immersed in continual life and death crises, without experiencing the reward of seeing that person vibrant and alive.

"Do you all know Barry?" I asked.

They certainly did, as his recovery was almost celebrity worthy.

"You know him?" Dr. Ghandi asked.

"By saving Barry, you saved the man who last spoke with my son. Barry's conversation with Marshall is instrumental in my not losing faith," I said.

"Do you know Ever?" I asked.

And with that, I told the full-circle story about Ever and Dr. Haynes. What I would have missed had I not looked back to say, "Thank you!"

I learned how rare it is that people ever come back to say those words. It's a privilege to witness another reaping their reward through the powerful act of gratitude. People rarely do things solely for the money or the recognition. They more want to make a positive difference. We, as recipients, rob them of their reward when we neglect to make them aware of how they impacted us. It's simple but powerful. When we hurt, we often want to hide from others. God moves through people. We shut God out when we shut ourselves off from others.

Moving forward, I hope to impact the rapidly growing suicide rate of our society. Hope Squad is an organization that is already successfully making a difference. Schools that implement this program claim remarkable success. Peer-to-peer training is an integral component of this youth suicide-prevention program. It trains the students to recognize warning signs in depressed or suicidal peers and empower them to properly give support and report certain warning signs to an adult. I'm thankful to The Jordan Elizabeth Harris Foundation for their work in getting this program into Texas schools.

Brain images are now available that could help us study the effects of habits. Brain images of a video game addict and how that same brain reacts when removed from a technically infused lifestyle effects visible changes. The behavior, psychological, and attitude changes were as significant as the images of change to that brain.

I also hope to encourage more research on the effects of trauma, porn, video games, social media, music, and different types of music versus playing sports and walking in nature. We have new technology that will allow us to study how our habits affect our brain that can lead to better care for our brains and healing from trauma. "Mental fitness" will hopefully be a common expression, teaching habits with answers for Hopelessly Stuck on how to process and combat attacks from Charming Impossibles. Mental fitness can be our future answer to the child suffering from bullies and mean girls on the playground, for the kind young man married to a Charming Impossible bride, for the wife of an abusive husband, and for the student, church member, or coworker under psychological attack.

* * *

Seeking solace, I open the devotional Ever gave me, randomly flipping to a page with a story of Corrie ten Boom. It was toward the end of her life, where she lived in a home in California that was given to her. A gentleman visitor said to her, "Isn't God good

Painted by Marshall his junior year in high school in art class 2014

to have provided you this beautiful home overlooking the ocean?" admiring it's majesty and beauty.

She said, "Yes, but God was good to me in Ravensbrück, too."1

Closing the devotional, I thought about how she lost all of her family in concentration camps. She was a sole survivor, suffering many atrocities I can't even begin to imagine. Looking back on our journey, I thought about the self-protected me in my youth trapped behind my own walls. As one young high school classmate said, "I see you, but I can't get to you through those glass walls."

He was correct. I was not only untouchable but lacking empathy, having never really suffered. I must say, I do like the me on this side of pain much better. I'm free to love others more deeply and feel joy much more deeply, too.

Marshall is at peace. We will miss him terribly. We will be with him again.

Until then, we still have living yet to do. At the loss of all loved lost ones, we choose to remember the good, polishing their halo

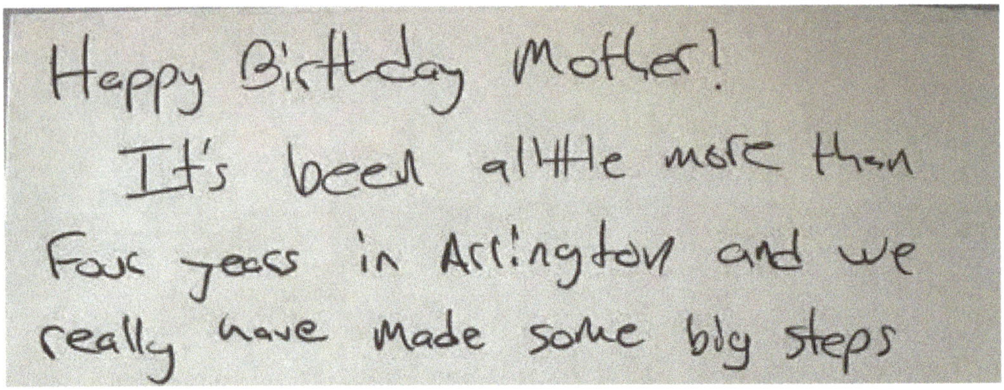

Happy Birthday Mother!
It's been alittle more than
Four years in Arlington and we
really have made some big steps

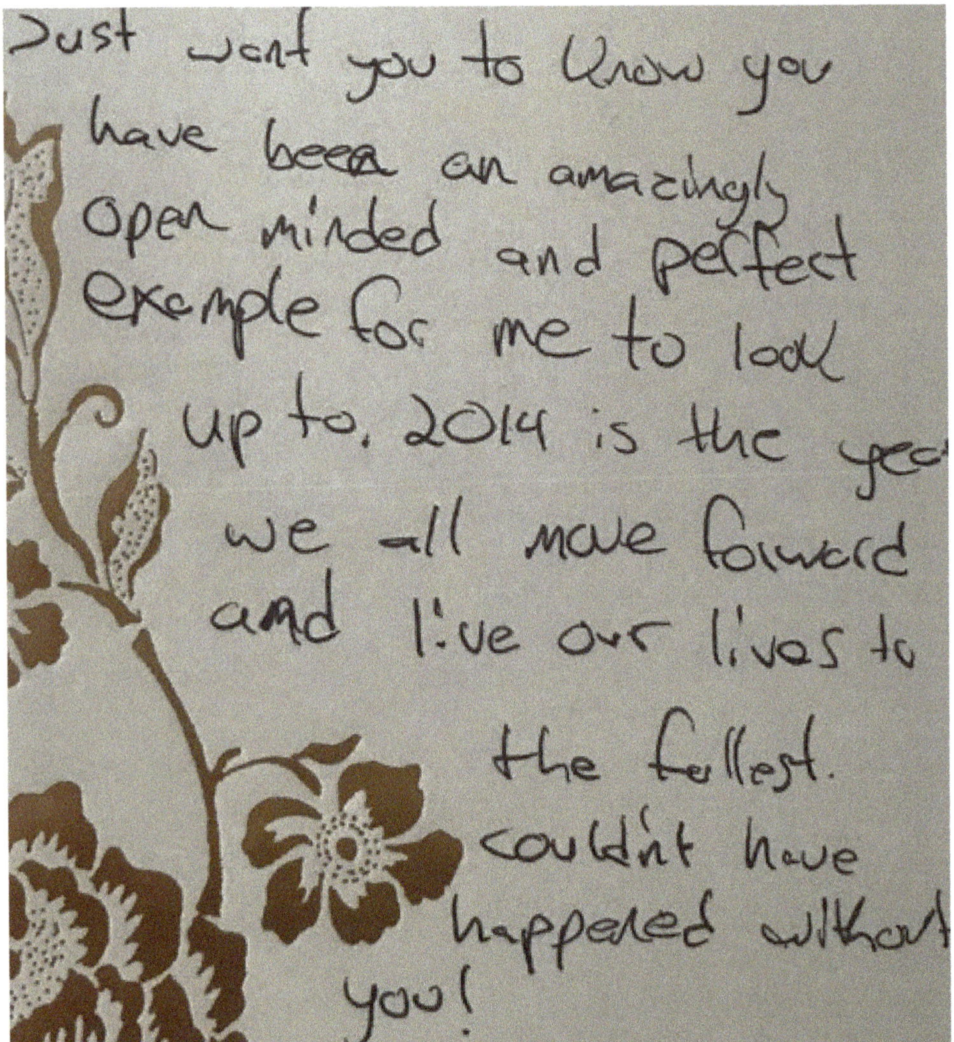

Just want you to know you
have been an amazingly
open minded and perfect
example for me to look
up to. 2014 is the year
we all move forward
and live our lives to
the fullest.
couldn't have
happened without
you!

This birthday message from Marshall reads: "It's been a little more than Four years in Arlington and we really have made some big steps. Just want you to know you have been an amazingly open minded and perfect example for me to look up to. 2014 is the year we all move forward and live our lives to the fullest. Couldn't have happened without you!"

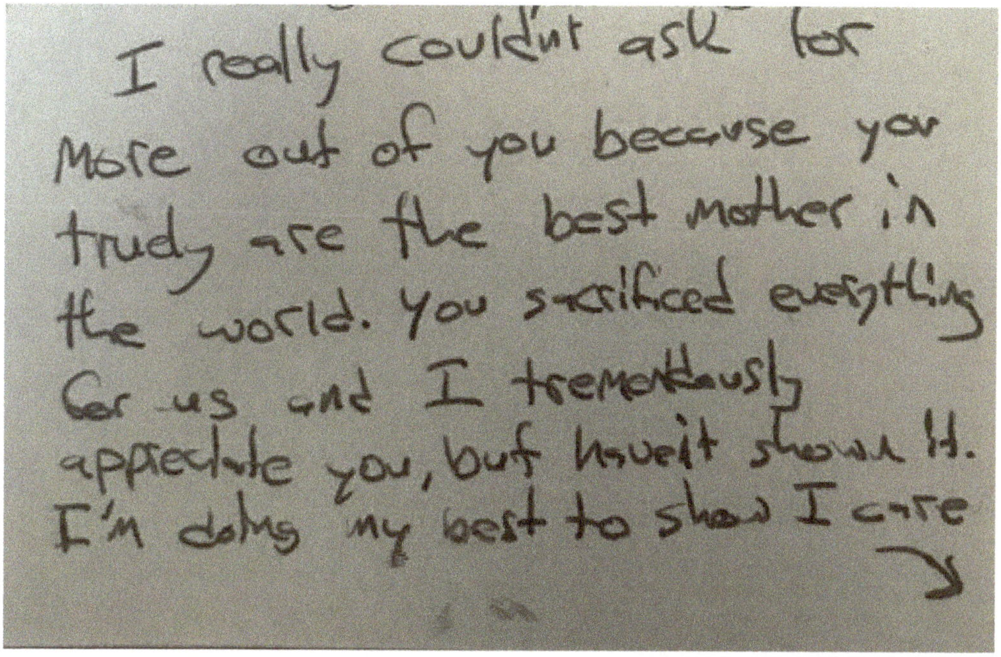

I really couldnt ask for
More out of you because you
truly are the best mother in
the world. You sacrificed everything
for us and I tremendously
appreciate you, but havent shown it.
I'm doing my best to show I care →

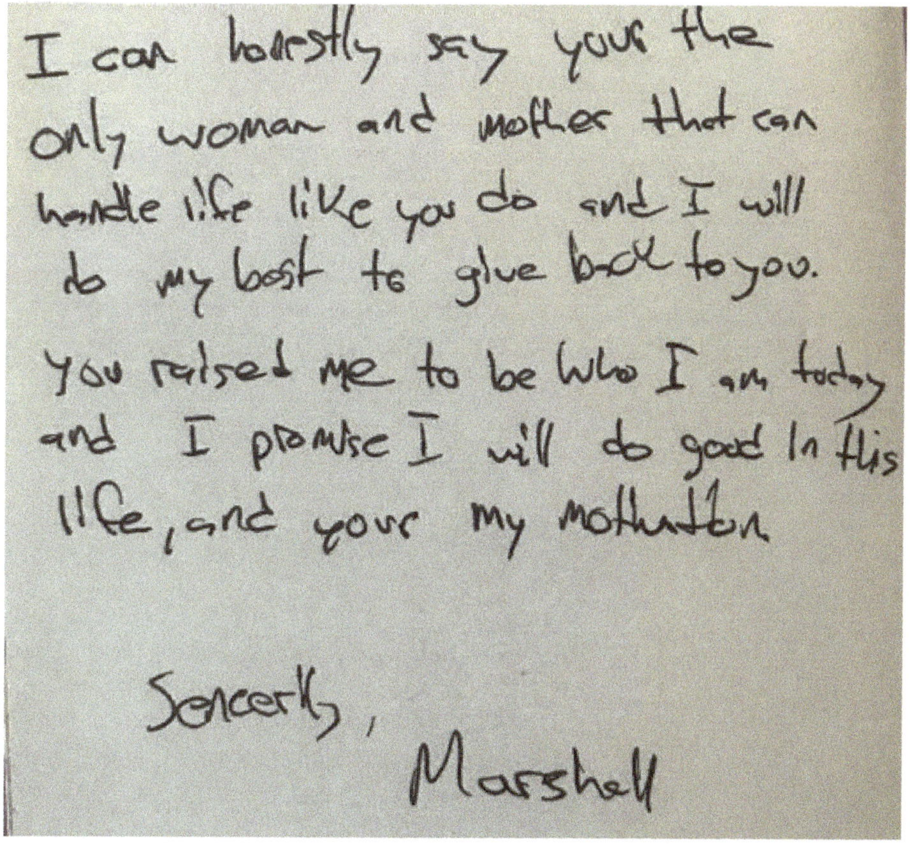

I can honestly say your the
only woman and mother that can
handle life like you do and I will
do my best to give back to you.
You raised me to be who I am today
and I promise I will do good in this
life, and your my mother

Sincerly,
Marshall

This card from Marshall reads: "I really couldn't ask for more out of you because you truly are the best mother in the world. You sacrificed everything for us, and I tremendously appreciate you, but haven't shown it. I'm doing my best to show I care. I can honestly say you're the only woman and mother that can handle life like you do and I will do my best to give back to you. You raised me to be who I am today and I promise I will do good in this life and you're my Mother!"
Sincerely, Marshall

a bit. It's what we do as humans: Losing a loved one who provided us many loving memories leaves a deep hole never to be filled in this life. My surviving children are true heroes to me. They have gone through much of what Marshall endured along with their own individual pain, plus the loss of a sibling. I applaud their courage, their dignity and grace. And of all four of them, I'm so very, very proud they maintain beautiful, loving hearts that remain tender towards others.

And just as Corrie said God was good in Ravensbrück, I see that through it all, God was, is, and always will be good.

Yes, indeed, God *is* good.

* * *

To my three surviving children and the too numerous to count other survivors of various abuses, remember: Many great people come from troubled homes and backgrounds. Together, let's choose to continue living our very best until God chooses to call us home.

I LOVE you sooo very much! Happy Birthday Mother!

Love,
Marshall

BE ALERT FOR NEW
OPPORTUNITIES IN BUSINESS
OR PLEASURE
PANDA EXPRESS • PANDA INN
Your eyes will soon be opened to a
world full of beauty, charm and adventure.
Lucky Numbers 49, 16, 55, 41, 46, 5

PART 4

Isiah Robertson invited me to participate in awarding a recipient of the Nancy Knaack Award of Excellence. For the full story, read Charming Impossibles: How Ordinary Angels Help Free the Hopelessly Stuck.

Nancy Anne Collins Knaack, affectionately known by her grandchildren as Nonnie, is my mother. She was also known as "Miss Nancy" to her many "sons" at House of Isaiah Drug and Alcohol Rehab where my mother volunteered for over 15 years. Founded by Isiah Robertson, NFL linebacker and six-time pro bowler, an overcomer from his own addiction, the award was established in her honor and given to a rare few. Isiah Robertson invited me to participate in giving out the Nancy Knaack Award of Excellence. Below, we are standing with the first recipient:

There are many reasons why Nancy Knaack was considered excellent. For me, it was my mother sitting on the edge of my bed at night regularly saying, "You need to pray for compassion."

Throughout her motherhood, she taught me through her actions—first, by taking my brother and me to nursing homes during our preschool years, just because. We drove along with our mother, taking a carload of the "elderly" bowling. With a cane in one hand and a bowling ball in another, they played and laughed like children. We sang along with our mother as she led them in sing-alongs. We went upstairs as she directed us to visit the one lady who would not come down to "join in the fun." Sometimes we laughed and sometimes we just quietly sat beside these lonely souls. I didn't understand until I was an adult why their eyes lit up when we walked in. At three and four years of age, I experienced that the gesture of simply showing up can bring joy. My brother and I were regular visitors until we were school-aged.

During our teen years, my mother invited many of her friends to our home. Many lived in other parts of town.

We drove with her to pick up her friends from parts of town we'd have otherwise never seen. One such friend spoke broken English. We would drive to Anna's apartment, pick her up, and take her to run errands. Usually, this included visiting her son, Paul, a grown man who talked to people we couldn't see. He scared me, but my mother and Anna treated him with great respect while teaching me about schizophrenia. My mother treated them both like they were special. She invited them to join us out to dinner and would volunteer me to assist them in carrying groceries into their home.

My mother hosted people in our home from every walk of life and every color and nationality. She loved them, admired them all, and taught me how to get to know and value a person's soul. They did not come into our home to serve us nor for her to serve them. She invited them in as friends. She didn't just welcome them, she wanted them. And she was always pleased and proud to introduce them to me.

Underneath my mother's joy and love loomed a battle with depression that she hid from me until my high school years. During her last years of life battling a lung condition that was later diagnosed as Sarcoidosis, while in hospice and under the care of extraordinary Ordinary Angels, a volunteer offered to help her write her story. Much of her focus was on mental health and what she learned and desired to pass onto others suffering with mental health issues.

Nancy went to heaven on Mother's Day, May 10, 2009. It was a perfect home going date for such a beloved woman who was a wonderful mother and grandmother to her own and to countless others.

Nancy's Story

In 2002, at the age of 63, I was diagnosed with pulmonary fibrosis, which is a life-threatening diagnosis. It was hard for me to accept because, generally speaking, I felt so good and so alive and had such plans for my future. I found myself in a quandary; I just didn't want to believe the doctors. I didn't feel that I was carrying that diagnosis, but I certainly wasn't going to try to prove the doctors wrong.

Because I was getting so frustrated, nervous, and confused, I just fell on my face and said, "Lord, you've got to help me. You've got to show me whether I have this disease or not. I'm asking you to take away the diagnosis of pulmonary fibrosis; heal me from the diagnosis."

I fervently prayed with every ounce of life in me. I was so afraid. The next morning, I arose from bed, and my breathing was tremendously improved. I said, "Thank you, I have been healed of pulmonary fibrosis."

I went to work believing I had really conquered the enemy. However, as time progressed, the symptoms did return, and they never really went away totally.

As I write this, I am 68. I'm pretty much housebound, and I'm on hospice. I can only walk 20 to 40 feet before I start breathing hard again. I don't have any pain: it's just extreme difficulty breathing. I don' t know where this will take me, or when the Lord will call me home, but I have made peace with my maker. I am ready to do His will in my life daily and look forward to going to heaven as a blessing, not as a curse.

During one visit with my doctor, he asked me about my childhood, and I responded that I could sum up my whole childhood, generally speaking, with one word: sadness. I could never understand where the sadness came from, why it was me, and what I did to bring it on. I just felt it must have been something I was thinking or doing that brought about this depression, but I couldn't put my finger on it. From the earliest of times, I remember the feeling of being on the outside of my family unit looking in at them happily living their lives as a family: my mother, father, sister, brother, and two grandmothers. I thought that was a strange word to use, "sadness," but as it came out of my mouth, I thought, It's true—I was always sad, even though we were a loving family, even though we had things that other people didn't have.

Recently, I learned of an advancement in the field of adolescent psychiatry and mental illness. Through a magazine or newspaper article, I learned that many children experience depression as early as infancy, and more commonly, as toddlers and adolescents, since they can express themselves better than infants. I got to thinking, That's the solution to the problem; my whole life was sadness.

Depression causes many different things, from emotional outbursts and fierce anger to fear. I experienced the extreme emotional outbursts and the anger, and I didn't know why; the least amount of change in a routine would throw me off-kilter. I was very argumentative, I was always right, and if somebody argued about that, then I would become very angry and would have one of my outbursts. I never felt I stood on firm ground. I always felt at any moment, the Earth could open up and I'd just slip down into the center of the Earth. The older I became, the more I was able to feel these episodes coming on and could isolate myself and calm myself down temporarily. However, I was never able to be relieved of that fear of saying the wrong thing, saying the right thing, fear of everything. I knew my family walked on eggshells around me. I didn't know why, and I didn't know how to change it.

I was born on October 21, 1939. I was a caesarian birth because of my mother's labor complications. Back in those days, you stayed in the hospital two weeks at least, and having had a caesarian, Mother stayed longer. They didn't know what to name me because they were expecting a boy, and the name they had chosen was Richard Lee. (Ironically, I went through school with a Richard Lee Collins. I always thought that was unusual.) The nurse said they had to pick a name soon or the hospital would name me. I couldn't leave the hospital without a name.

One night while going over names, my mom said, "Nancy Anne Collins," so that's what they named me. I love my name. I came home to a family of two toddlers. My sister was 20 months old and my brother was three and a half years old. I was born in Rock Island, Illinois.

My father had his own business. He was a plumbing contractor, and he was in business with Roy Brashar. My mom was a stay-at-home mom, as were most women in those days. Women then didn't have any electronic appliances to speak of other than a washing machine, which consisted of an agitator that cleaned the clothes, but it wasn't automatic. She had to turn it on and off and hand wring the water out of the clothes with a wringer. This occurred in the basement, which had a dirt floor and cinder block sides. (Homes in those days were very basic.) Then she would have to carry the baskets of laundry out to the backyard and pin it on a clothesline to dry.

My mother, having three children in diapers, had her hands full just taking care of the children. They say I tended to cry a lot. I know that I had a lot of illnesses. I was frequently sick and required extra attention. Of course, we didn't have medications in those days like we do today. You pretty much just had to work it out until the infection cleared itself up.

When I was two and a half, Mother was scrubbing the kitchen floor on her hands and knees, and we kept begging her to go to the store, which was a block down from our house. It was an ice cream store which also had their own fine chocolates. They also had penny candy, and we would stand and look over the goodies for what would seem like hours when we got a few pennies together. On this occasion, my mother gave my sister some money. We walked down to the comer. My sister said she would look for cars coming, and when the time was right, I would cross the street. When I walked across the street, I was hit by a car. I sustained multiple head injuries, including a fractured jaw and a number of stitches. I ended up with two black eyes, and I remember my brother and sister laughing at me. They said I looked like a monkey.

Shortly after the car accident, my mother became very ill and was hospitalized. My father had to continue working, so my brother, the oldest, was sent to stay with a relative while my sister and I were sent to an orphanage. It was a very traumatic experience for me to be separated from my mother so young. Upon our return, I remember my mother crying over us as she shampooed our hair over the sink washing out lice.

We began to outgrow our house, and by the time I was 10, my father had built us a brand-new house up on the hill. We thought it was so huge. It looked to us like a big plantation house. Today, we drive by and marvel and laugh at how small it really is. It was new, and we got new furniture, and it seemed like the start of a new life for all of us. My brother started junior high school, and my mother became active in school activities.

It was at that time that we joined the Episcopal church as a family. We loved the church and took a very active part. My sister and I sang in the children's choir, my brother was an acolyte, or candle bearer, and Mother was involved with the women' s group that cooked for different occasions. My father was on the vestry.

My parents had married very young, and there was some early trauma in their lives in that my grandfather passed away by suicide when my father was just 21 years old. My grandfather's death was rarely mentioned or talked about. My parents went from being newlyweds living a quiet, normal life to living with my grandmother, Nonnie, in a one-bedroom apartment.

Nonnie worked all day and was very active in the Shriner's and was gone many evenings. When she came home, she would have to walk through my parents' sleeping area to get to her bedroom. This caused a bit of apprehension on the part of my mother. However, they soon did fall into a routine.

My father was a very funny man. He had a great sense of humor and loved to tell long stories that were going nowhere just to end up with a corny ending, and he'd laugh louder than we would. He was very funny and could be very entertaining, loving being the center of attention.

But he also had a sharp temper. His responses of anger I often didn't see coming nor did I understand. His angry outbursts often confused me. He played a big part in Santa Claus, the Easter Bunny, and those holidays where fairy tales and drama were involved. My mother was loving and peaceful. She would sit back, allowing my dad to take over.

When I was a junior in high school, I went to special classes to become a nurse's aide to assist nurses in the local hospital, and we were allowed to work on Saturdays. I loved that work. I loved working in the medical field, and I especially loved working with nurses and staff. I would take temperatures, and I would bathe incoming patients. I would deliver food trays, and it was just very exciting to me. Other summers in high school, I worked as a camp counselor through the YWCA. We had boating, canoeing, outdoor camping and cooking, handicrafts, and archery. Counselors took turns teaching the different classes. I loved them all. We also took each cabin on an overnight camp/cookout once a week. It was a very special time for any young child to have the opportunity to do these things. I felt very lucky to be in a city where they provided this for us. I learned a lot working as a counselor.

In February 1958, I enrolled in the American Institute of Commerce (AIC) in Davenport, Iowa, to study business practices and secretarial skills. During this time, I became acquainted with Rodger Knaack. He was in his first year of studies at AIC and beginning his second year of advanced business skills and advanced accounting. His goal was to become a certified public accountant. Prior to this, Rodger had completed two years of college, until his GI bill funds ended. He then took on two part¬-time jobs to pay for his studies at AIC and for room and board at his parents' house.

Rodger was born in Burlington, Iowa, and had an older sister. They frequently moved around Iowa because his father was a traveling salesman with Standard Oil Company and was developing his territory. Rodger developed good work skills because his folks told him if he wanted anything (be it a basketball, bicycle, or car), he would need to find a job to pay for it. As a result, he was very thrifty with his money.

We dated for a few years and got married in May of 1960 at Trinity Episcopal Church in Rock Island, Illinois, where I had grown up and attended church all my life. When Rodger completed his schooling and graduated from AIC, he decided against becoming a CPA and went into sales like his father had done. He really enjoyed that contact with people and the challenge of selling products. He interviewed with the Wrigley Company and got his first job and territory.

Rodger and I started a family with the birth of a son born in the fall of 1962. He was, named after his two grandfathers. Our second child, Susan Elizabeth, was born in the summer of 1964. Our family has always been a very close-knit family. We've always supported each other in both good and bad times. One of the fundamental things that has kept us a tight-knit family group is our belief in God.

Although I worked in the field of medicine, mainly psychiatry, as a medical secretary, it never clicked with me that the sadness I suffered since my childhood, which continued into adulthood, could be depression. I guess it's so subtle that you think you're making it up. So, instead of thinking that I had a disease that needed to be treated, I thought that I was making it up and just wanted attention.

When I was about 50, I woke up one morning as I normally would and got ready for work. With outside circumstances adding to my sadness involving my daughter's marriage, I one day thought, Oh hell, I can't do this anymore. I went to the medicine cabinet where I had an old bottle of sleeping pill samples. I went out to the kitchen, opened the capsules, stirred up the powder of 32 capsules with water, and gulped it down. It was the strangest feeling.

Initially, it felt like I had won the battle. That immediately was followed by remorse, but I had done it, and I lay down on the floor with my pillow and began to pray. I said, "Lord, forgive me for what I've just done. I know it's a sin in your eyes to commit suicide. And I hold myself totally responsible for this. I'm honestly not sorry I did it, even though I know it was wrong, but I just can't go on like this and I hope you will forgive me. I want to spend eternity with you. But I'll never make it if l go on. I guess I' m taking my chances that you'll forgive me, so that I can spend eternity with you. If not, I will have to suffer the consequences."

Next thing I knew, I woke up in a hospital room, bright-eyed and, and I called for a nurse. She came in and then sent for the doctor. He asked if I knew what I had done, and I told him, "Yes." He asked, "Are you ever going to try this again?" I said, "No." He stated, "Then I can release you to a doctor's care, so you need to contact a psychiatrist and get some help." I said, " Okay."

I was so depressed, I couldn't think of anybody but myself. I didn't think of how it would affect my husband, my parents, my children, or any of my friends or family. It would be so much easier to know that you were sad and that it was "okay" to go to a psychiatrist or counselor. The stigma of mental illness has been such an albatross around the neck of society and such a taboo; whereas, the alternative, suicide, is a far worse outcome. I had not talked to my family, though I had been going to counseling. Just prior to this, my counselor had said, "Will you make a pact with me, that if you feel this way you won't do anything, but will call me?" I said, "Sure," but I thought that if somebody wants to take their own life, they won' t tell anybody. I am so grateful for the opportunity to face my disease and find someone who would help me through this. I remember walking down the hallway of a medical practice, and on the wall were pictures of all the different doctors. I hoped for one doctor, and when he came into the exam room, you could have knocked me over with a feather. That reinforced my belief that this whole situation was God-driven. He heard my prayer. I should have died, but instead, I got an understanding doctor, and we had a wonderful rapport.

He asked about my childhood. As a child, I went through the mumps, the measles, chicken pox, and whooping cough. Healing this disease was a lot harder than anything I've ever been through, but I stuck with it. I was honest with myself and the doctor. We tried every psychotropic drug available, and some that were brand new. They would work for maybe a month, six weeks, then they would even out, and I would go back down into the slump. Well, this doctor decided to close his private practice, so I had to look for another one. I was working in an organization that used a psychiatrist for our young clients, and I often drove them to their appointments. Therefore, I began to have a working relationship with this doctor, and so I called him, and he took me as a client. We continued the quest for the right combination of medications, and it was years before I found the correct one. The doctor said, "I've never used this combination before, but from what you're saying it sounds like you need another drug to balance out these others. So, I'm going to try you on this new combination and see how you do." I knew immediately that this combination was going to work. It not only worked, but it took the weight of the world off my shoulders. It took away all that living in the hellish state of severe "sadness." Mind you, this whole time I appeared to others as a fun-loving, silly, outgoing person that always had a joke to tell. Nobody knew that I was depressed because I didn't even think I was depressed.

It was a long road to recovery, and it is also one that never ends. It took about six years for me finally to find the correct balance of medications, and suddenly, I had a sense of well-being. I was happy most of the time instead of sad. I could handle stress much more easily. So, I began celebrating new life for the first time in my whole life.

There's no question in my mind that God was with me the whole time. I thank Him from the bottom of my heart. My quest is to share my story with other people who might be depressed. For so many years, depression was unknown, and then for so many years, it was a closet disease. You didn't talk about it.

I wholeheartedly encourage anybody who thinks they might be "just sad" to go to a counselor and/or a psychiatrist. They have tests they can give you that immediately tell you if there's an inkling of depression there. When I took the test in the hospital, I checked "yes" to everything from the first day. I never had even thought about those questions. Nobody in my family had ever known anybody with deep depression that I know of. But I must remember that my father' s father shot himself when my father was 21 years of age. That shows there was some underlying depression in that part of the family.

When I finally got on the right medications, I felt like God had just put his hand on my shoulder and said, "My daughter, you are healed." I remain in this state of happiness to this very day, January 8, 2009.

I believe in the adage "Don't judge another person until you've walked a mile in his shoes." I leave you with this thought: "Judge not, that ye be not judged." Take a long, hard look at that because we're all going to be judged one day. I want to make amends before God, just for the pure sake of peace in my heart. If you' re going to judge others, you believe they will judge you, and it makes for a very unhealthy, unhappy life story. All through my life, the ribbon of thought, "Let go, and let God," has been an active part of my belief system. I wish you love, peace, and joy.

—Nancy Knaack

Marshall's Siblings

Marshall's Oldest Sister

All my siblings feel like a natural extension of me. They each bring out certain sides of me. The mother, the friend, the life of the party, the creative, the naturalist, the empath . . . the big sister. It always feels like we all need to be together all the time. One-on-one situations feel funny or odd. It feels right and best when we are all together. I identify with each of my siblings, in each of their different phases, in the strangest but most natural way. At times it feels like nobody can get under my skin the way a sibling can. And it fascinates me how I tend to get so raw with my siblings . . . but I think it's because they are the extension of me that sometimes isn't what I want to see. Because we have always been such a team, I could never imagine living without one of them.

At one point in our lives, Marshall was the little brother goober that always managed to draw blood in some freak accident, hardly ever showing fear or pain. In other phases of our lives, he was the deviant entrepreneur breaking all the rules and writing his own. At other times he was the philosopher. I identified with him, in each phase, in various ways. Marshall was my little brother who fought everything: expectations, standards, tradition, stereotypes, injustice, depression . . . and ultimately, he made a choice. His decision left us with choices that had to be made as survivors of a lost extension of ourselves. Whom do we become now?

There were many times after Marshall passed that I felt complete guilt. I felt that I should have devoted more of myself to my family than selfishly focusing on getting better. I genuinely thought I failed him and my family. But I know now that there is no way I could be of any help to my family, friends, or even strangers, until I first loved myself and built a strong foundation from which I could grow and give to others. Looking back, I know how many times I did reach out, asking him to please follow me on my path. I offered to have him room with me in Dallas and see what I was doing with my life . . . begging him to give it a shot. I saw how it was changing my reality, and I urged him to explore this option with me. He would always find a reason to not accept. I know he wanted to, but there was always something keeping him from taking the leap of faith.

I've accepted that he made his choices. But, truthfully, I will never be able to say to myself or to anyone that I couldn't have done more. Of course, I could, which leaves me now to simply try to continue pouring love, strength, and support into anyone I can.

Recently I found myself driving through the city where we began the new life of just us five. I was with my fiancé, Matt, heading to see my mom on her birthday when I told Matt how odd, almost unreal, it felt to pass the exit to our old duplex where we began our new life years ago. It was undoubtedly the worst, most utterly tragic, terrible chapter of my life. It felt like we were going through emotional chemotherapy. There, we fully embraced the lows. We let ourselves die enough to eliminate the old toxic past without going so far as to kill us. We hung on to life with and for each other. We had to as no way in this world could we make it without each other, together.

At that time in my life, I could not fathom feeling as happy and completely blessed as I do now. I couldn't imagine having a clear head devoid of the nuclear waste of my past. I couldn't imagine ever having a partner in life who knew about my lows; appreciated my past, present and future aspirations; and who wanted to be with me more than anything. I couldn't imagine ever being able to be with my siblings and not feel pain. Today, all of those seemingly unattainable dreams are my reality. And it required a lot of work to get here.

Life is all about choices. Sure, there are events that are out of our control, but we are always in the driver seat of how we respond. I made a choice in college to get the hell out of this funk. I would not let this life keep me down. I knew that I needed to keep my mind and body strong or this wouldn't be possible. I dove headfirst into physical fitness. I tried a lot of different approaches discovering what worked for me and fulfilled me.

First, I wouldn't sacrifice my workout routine or diet for anything or anyone. It was necessary to stay fit enough to fight through the emotional battles I was fighting. Second, I kept my focus on the people who were helping me become who I wanted to be, the people who poured love and strength into me, who didn't drain me. After a few years, I found myself pouring into others. I found myself actually helping others. It was a wild realization for me when I recognized that I had broken through a threshold. I can't even say when that actually happened. It was a slow process, not a defining moment. But one day I realized, Oh shit, I'm like, better now!

I do not have it all figured out. I can say, however, that I am not full of regret. I have managed to build a life in which I am happy. The universe was kind enough to allow me to meet wonderful, beautiful, genuine, kind people who love on me and grow with me. I

had to work on myself, long and hard, to be able to attract these people and recognize this. It required daily choices to recognize the good in the world around me. I think Marshall didn't allow enough time in his life to get to that point. He was too impatient.

But I am here now. Love is the answer, people over possessions. Know thyself: What feeds your soul and what drains it. It's important to know both so that you can navigate all the pandemonium that life throws your way. Trust me, the pandemonium never stops coming, but that is not a reason to quit. I can honestly say, "Life is good." There was a long period of my life where I wouldn't dare dream that was possible. We must keep moving forward and keep making the difficult choices that will get us to the other side. We all have the opportunity to thrive. We just need to keep pushing ourselves forward.

Marshall's Brother

We called him a "gentle giant."

Marshall Foster to me is my little brother, someone I love. I look back with regret at certain times in our lives, thinking of how much more I could have included him in my life. With a nearly four years' difference in age, a wider relationship gap existed at times. Consistent, however, throughout our childhood and into our later years is our playing video games together. Video games connected Marshall and me no matter the age gap, no matter if I was off at college or we were living across town from each other in separate apartments. This remained something we did together quite often, too. On N64 and later on Xbox, we created many memories that I cherish.

Outdoorsmen through and through, we liked a lot of the same things. We four siblings as kids were always outside playing together in the river, in the field, in the mud, you name it; we were playing . . . together. We all were hardworking, too, focused until the job was done. With any task, one of us would know how to figure it out, and the rest of us could understand the "devised" plan. I never noticed it until after Marshall passed, but we took great pride in ourselves when we were together. We were a good team, and a force to be reckoned with in any situation.

In his later life, Marshall became a true young man, tall and strong with a kind yet sure-footed presence. I was very fortunate to be able to spend most of my time with Marshall and his friends. It was with this group that I began to see my little brother as a friend and a man of his own. Shout out to the "Shedboyz!" as we called ourselves. I am so incredibly grateful to them for those times I got to camp out with my little brother, just being young and wild, whether in nature, hanging out by the campfire, or just hanging around inside . . . just being. Very quickly he stopped being just my little brother; he soon became someone I trusted and revered as an individual. His mind was very open and analytical, always looking for answers, leaving no room for guessing. We would talk for hours about our beliefs, our questions about this crazy life: all of those existential questions we ask ourselves but never truly answer. Our life, growing up together in particular, brought many questions . . . questions we were not equipped to answer for ourselves. And that was troubling, especially for Marshall.

Truth was paramount to him and that's how he lived, taking everything at face value, never being very judgmental until he'd discover a basis from which to judge. At which point, my brother had an all-or-nothing mentality that I believe helped in many crossroads in his life yet hurt him so much more effectively when he was vulnerable. He and I both dealt with our own forms of depression, and talking about it together wasn't easy. We opened up sometimes, usually speaking in vague, unsure metaphors, attempting vulnerability, eventually laughing it off, and changing the subject to something less "colossal." Unresolved pain from our childhood was very present in all our lives; we all also knew, very well, how to hide it. More attention to it just meant more stress, more self-inflicted guilt, and more pain. All of which we actively avoided, for our own self-health. Marshall and I avoided it also "for" our sisters and mother. We talked about suicide together fairly often in the end, eventually coming to the conclusion that we couldn't leave our girls behind or even do that to them. We talked about how it would suck to have to live without one of them. How little I knew about how much that would hurt.

Finding him was the most surreal experience I've ever had in my life. My mom called me that morning worried about Marshall; this wasn't the first time I had been awakened by my terrified mother. She had known more than even I did about his depression. This time that she called, I felt I should go support Marshall. I expected to find him fed up and angry at life, not wanting to answer his phone, definitely not wanting us banging on his door, trying to talk. But this time was different. His windows we screwed shut, the outside patio locked, door bolted, and worse, he wasn't answering me. So many thoughts crossed my mind, but never actually suicide. It couldn't be, not my brother. After all, he always said he would one day be the cool "Uncle Marshall." I'm going to see that crazy dude get old, fall in love, and do more stupid things with me, I reassured myself.

My mother insisted on breaking into my brother's apartment that was deadbolt locked from within. Management requested police be present. And my mother was unsuccessful at getting their approval to break in due to privacy laws. Marshall was 21. He was considered an adult.

"Fine," my mother responded to them. "You may leave. I'll break in when you are gone," she said. "My son is in there. And I'm going in to help him."

To the manager she asked, "Do you want me to go through the glass door, window, or main door? I'll pay for the repairs."

With their backs toward us, revealing no "official" approval, the police stood as the apartment maintenance man directed my close friend Ian and me on how to kick in the door. On the third try, we looked at each other breaching the entryway of a dark room where my brother's body lay on the couch. My first thought was literally, How did you sleep through all of that? It quickly changed when I saw Ian turn back toward the door to my mother. Then I saw a revolver at my brother's side. I remember it so vividly . . . sometimes as a simple memory that passes by and other times unexpectedly bringing me to my knees literally, without warning or remorse. I remember not even being capable of fathoming the thought that he wasn't in there.

My siblings and I were very lost for a while. We had faced hard times before and we were there for each other, but this was a true test. Up until Marshall's passing, by choice, my memory of our past was usually very positive and happy. I was always lucky enough to be surrounded by good friends, true friends. I now realize, those happy memories were/are a fortunate escape from the actual battlefield of our home life.

Today I'm left with no escape from the loss of my little brother. I can't go anywhere to see him; the cemetery is too quiet. I have to face that sad void every day, which brings me to a place where I see depression as a choice, a crossroads rather than a result of my "misfortune." I can do something about it. I can and have fought back, discovering the possibility of peace and happiness again. Still, I feel anguish as well. It's a miserable loss that I believe will never leave, but I get the chance to feel myself heal more and more every day.

The tragic loss of my brother, Marshall, has forced me to realize the impact that everyone has on each other in this life and that I have on my surroundings. We are all brothers and sisters, and your loss hurts me, everyone you know and don't know. Now I realize that my leaving would have only pushed my problems onto my siblings, which could never rid me of my own. Of course my emotions increased after his death, as did my awareness of my own depression. Crying became normalized very quickly in my life, a welcome flow forcing me to face my emotions and pain. Crying became a great release that I had previously withheld from myself. We were all taught, inaccurately, that it was weak and almost unnecessary in most situations. Crying is unavoidable now and gives me a chance to open up to myself and to those close to me, bringing a sense of peace.

Having people near helping me deal with my loss has been integral, as friends help me take a break from my pain. I'm a homebody, I needed time alone, but independence eventually can turn to seclusion. I am grateful for friends around inviting me out even though I may be just a quiet, sad presence; friends who would not take no for an answer when I was truly down.

Some people, like my best friend, TJ, played both roles in my life. He was there for me, somehow always knowing just how to lift my spirits, whether to sit and listen or get me out away from it all. He has been a constant in my life, a foundation that I could lean on. I'm very grateful for TJ.

I look forward more and more to new days ahead as I allow myself to face the past and then continue to let it pass on. By adopting the mindset of I get the chance to live every day, I'm creating a new life for myself that I still struggle with but find comfort and pride in as well. Pride that I am a warrior, that I show kindness and compassion when I could wallow in self-pity. Without these trials, I would not have discovered my own strength, proving capabilities to myself, or experiencing the power of vulnerability. I've chosen to love, without expectation or anticipation, as much as I can. In this self-discovery, I have a greater awareness when making life choices. I'm recognizing greater understanding that is gained and possible only through loss. Death left a sting that in its own excruciating way is also becoming a blessing, a chance to grow myself and help others.

It's still hard. It's painful at times. Some days I don't even want to leave my bed. This life seems an apparent test of some sort. In choosing to see beauty and to remain fascinated in the "small" things, I realize that this life has something to offer me. And I want it.

The potential of life yet lived is the adventure that drives me today. Problems with grips and pulls are inevitable and may be cause for that dark place to revisit. What keeps me hopeful is knowing that I'm not alone. There are others who feel my pain, more pain, worse pain than I can imagine. I hope to show those others that they aren't alone either. For those next to me, for the ones who can't "see" anyone next to them, and for the ones we've lost like my little brother, our "gentle giant," I want to live my purpose and possibly inspire another to choose life and trust in the fact that there is always *hope*.

Self-Discovery

by CF IV

I've discovered myself.
That there is more to life than working a job
For someone courageous enough to create their own.
That the body and soul I carry
Encumbers whatever I allow it to.
That my worth is defined by myself
By what I demand from my surroundings.
My presence is my effect,
And the fact that I expect nothing offers nothing.
Nothing but an empty hand extended for compensation
Of a job not completed nor attempted.
The belief that I am worthless offers nothing.
Nothing but shame and defeat;
A miserable existence that which I could never retire,
Bringing a long and sufferable life of unfulfilled voids.
There is, however, a boundless ability inside of me
that could reach for the stars and take grip.

A big part of me that yearns for adventure,
the flame I let no one see.
It's all I have left, I think to myself.
I've disrespected myself long enough
Believing someone else could claim that.
My fears take hold so tightly
I've become accustomed to their embrace.
This loving crutch I've become.
My harshest critic,
I've demanded the impossible of myself without remorse,
without a chance at satisfying my need for fulfillment.
This lack of pursuit
further deepening my sense of loneliness and distress
leaving me surrounded yet alone in my mind.
I choose this.
Every moment of bombardment of choice confronts me
and with pride I face the monster within.
Never failing to fight for others and their dream,
only to fail at my own.
I have discovered myself,
and I should be tired of looking the other way.

Marshall's Middle Sister

Being the younger two of four siblings, Marshall and I shared the same innocent mind that craved adventure and sought to discover the world together. We learned how to ride bikes together, that snakes aren't always as friendly as they appear, that he loved salsa and I wasn't a fan, and other goofy memories like those. In our early years, Marshall and I were always two peas in a pod; people often thought we were twins. I remember the day it all changed for Marshall, when he shifted from this shy, sweet boy to a boy full of pain and anger. Why I have such vivid recollections of our past I couldn't say for sure.

I carry a heavy burden through my memory. As a young child not understanding the ways of the world, I maintained a sense of curiosity. I wanted to understand why the things being done to each of us were happening. Being provided a perverted excuse or justification by the one person in our lives who promised to protect us above all was clouding my understanding of what was good and what was bad. Everything we faced, how we were treated, the twisted forms of discipline, and everything else that shaped our childhood were not normal, but it was our normal. We didn't know any different, nor was questioning openly allowed. Something felt off to me. So I was always observing, recording in my mind, and watching.

I reached a point in my life that led to a fork in the road. For me to truly find any healing, I had a very important decision to make. I could continue down the road of confusion, solitude, and bitterness, or I could choose the harder road that would eventually uncover the sources of my pain, open up the locked boxes in my mind, and scariest of all, face everything that had been hidden away. To truly gain back parts of myself that had been locked away for so many years required me to choose to deal with the darkest memories inside of me. While I am glad, now, to have made that choice, it took many difficult years to finally reach a place in my life where I felt I had strong footing. Feeling a sense of self-assuredness came late in life, for me. Because this process required the ability to remember some of my earliest memories, I believe that while my pain stems from having vivid memory of not only my own trauma but also that of all my family, it was and is key to my healing as well.

I believe Marshall had reached a similar crossroads and genuinely wanted to heal and get past the pain that burdened him every day. Unfortunately, he chose to stop fighting back against everything inside that was tearing him apart. I too had thoughts of leaving all this pain behind and not having to feel it anymore. In my eyes, the thought of suicide provided a twisted appearance of peace that at the time our lives were definitely lacking. I now understand what choosing life truly offers and wish my baby brother would've fought just a little longer because I believe he was close to finding a level of peace here in the world with his siblings by his side.

I was angry for a long time for the decision he made and for how badly I felt knowing he was gone forever. I just thought I'd see him get married and have a bunch of kids who acted just like he did. I thought we would all grow old together and laugh about the things we did as kids surrounded by our own. I have come to believe that he is never truly gone. I believe he is watching over us, that a part of him remains in each of us, and we will carry him with us forever.

We Foster siblings have always been a force. While always strongest together, we each provide an aspect of support or character that completes one another. As one stone alone can be difficult to break, add several more and you can create an impenetrable wall. I believe we each similarly have drawn strength from the pain of our past, and that is making each of us stronger. All together, the world doesn't stand a chance to ever break us again.

I am proud of each of my siblings, and there is no one I hold in higher respect than them. There isn't anyone who will ever understand me like they do and vice versa. We were in the trenches together, and even though we have been weakened by the greatest loss we have ever experienced, we have also come out stronger than ever. We may not be fully whole, but Marshall is always with us, watching from above and smiling.

Marshall's Mother

After Marshall's passing, and following the phase of regularly awaking every night in a panic-stricken litany of "should ofs or could haves," I settled into awaking every morning from a restless sleep to immediate tears flowing across my pillow. I had moved from chronic self-analysis to the deepest, heaviest sadness I had ever felt.

Honestly, my mind became absorbed with the desire to jump into the grave with my son. I longed to be with him, wherever he was. And I could not imagine living the rest of my life here on this Earth without him. That was way too much to bear. I wanted away from here. I wondered, Are we going to make it through this? Do I even want to? Will I lose another one to suicide? How do we ever get to the other side of this trauma, this hell of a life we've been enduring? Why continue to endure? And for what do we continue? Life was beginning to feel utterly meaningless, hopeless, and certainly not worth the pain. Grief took me to a place of self-absorption, which led me to believing, I don't care how this may affect others; I want to end this pain at any cost. I felt that Marshall deserved for me to grieve his loss. For the first time in my life, I understood how Marshall could do "it." I understood how my mother could "try." It was horribly tempting.

While the girls built emotional walls isolating themselves to grieve privately, my oldest son softened sharing his tears, his sorrow, and his misery with me. I knew we each would grieve in our own way and it would be important to embrace those differences. Marshall's brother and I cried a lot together. He and I allowed each other to cry, to feel sad, and to openly say that we didn't want to be here voicing how hopeless we felt. We understood one another's desperation and longing to be with Marshall. We missed him so. And we agreed that life can be so hellish—why keep trying?

Deep grief revealed to me an even deeper layer of just how easy it is to lie to myself, to believe my own lies, and to hide my own truth. This human behavior, which can start out as self-protective, can nevertheless manifest itself through debilitating anger and jealousy, illnesses like eating disorders, and even death. Until I reached this level of grief, I never realized that it was my own inner voices, my inner "demons," from whom I needed to escape. I realized, once again, that only truth could set me free.

This realization motivated me to seek healing. I wanted to go deep within, as deep as my sorrow. But this time, it wouldn't be to wallow in it, but rather to face, feel, and experience it. I also knew that any pain of mine left unaddressed would only emerge later. So by dealing with the deepest pain immediately, I hoped to avoid having it creep up later from behind. I chose not to medicate it, not to try to counsel it away, not to avoid it, but rather to face it, feel it, and embrace it. It was dark, it was scary, and at times it felt frighteningly

permanent. In the beginning of my search, I could not find any peace. In fact, my lack of peace only grew worse. But I kept seeking.

While flying through clouds to the Colorado mountains, peering from the window, I wondered if I was closer to Marshall. "Am I closer to you up here?" I asked him, at which point my gaze turned from the cloud puffs outside my window to the American Way magazine in the seat pocket in front of me. Opening it, my eyes fell on an article about Sisters First, a book written by Barbara and Jenna Bush. The short article highlighted that Barbara, while in high school, lost a boyfriend to suicide and that later in her life still sought unmet closure. The article went on to reveal that Barbara disguised herself and visited a medium with a photo of her old boyfriend. Barbara received closure that day. Reading her story inspired me to do the same.

My oldest daughter joined me in visiting a medium. While driving to the appointment, I said to her, "I'm looking forward to getting my hair cut and highlighted tomorrow." It was a simple comment, just making conversation. Together, we arrived at our appointment, agreeing to conceal our names, our emotions, and why we were visiting.

Immediately, we were informed that we had lost a loved one prematurely and that it was gun related. As the medium continued sharing facts we knew to be true that were impossible for him to know, I remained skeptical.

Until, that is, the medium asked, "Who is getting their hair cut and highlighted tomorrow?"

My first response, of any sort, was, "I am!"

He continued, "Well, your son is laughing because he can never tell the difference."

"Mom, that's Marshall!" my daughter said, chuckling, breaking her silence. "That was a secret joke among us siblings," she explained. "We all joked about how funny it is that you get so excited about getting your hair cut and highlighted and we can never tell the difference. That's him, Mom!" his sister proclaimed. "That's Marshall!"

With no knowledge of our conversation on way to the appointment, the medium continued. "Well," said the medium, "he was with you in your car on the way up here and he'll be with you on your way back. And he will be with you tomorrow when you get your hair done."

For an hour, my daughter and I experienced an undeniable connection to Marshall. We were both so grateful to have witnessed the connection together, because our experience would have been hard to believe or tell otherwise. For each of us, it was healing. This encounter with my son is essential to my peace of mind. I will forever remain grateful for the gift I received from the medium that day.

Finally, I was beginning to find peace for myself and, with that, acceptance of Marshall's choice. One day, I awoke without tears. It happened organically. Eventually, my son came over to visit, and we didn't cry. Not immediately, anyway. Without any clear explanation, laughter returned, followed by a quick slap of guilt. With sad eyes, we nevertheless did begin to smile. Gradually, my eyes smiled, too, as the guilt and sadness began to subside. Marshall would not have wanted us grieving. He deserved our joy much more.

We talked about visiting Marshall at the cemetery, how we envisioned crying out our pain there, but once we arrived, no release of emotion ever happened. We'd go separately and sometimes together, anticipating some sense of relief, closeness, something. But we both experienced little or nothing. Marshall wasn't there. Visiting the cemetery felt devoid of comfort, though we felt it was respectful and the right thing to do. Driving by his old apartment was heavy. The pain only worsened there. Struggling to navigate this great divide between my son who had passed on and me, my heart ached continually, albeit with short lapses of relief.

Like life, grieving and healing is a process, a journey. It's more about how we respond on the road toward a destination rather than about arriving. Grieving is messy and ugly. Healing requires patience, time, lots of talking, tears, angry outbursts, and sitting still, quietly.

My self-pity began to melt as I focused more on those I do have here on Earth rather than those I do not. Meeting with a medium and receiving the convincing gift of connection to Marshall helped me to accept that Marshall's choice doesn't take away from my purpose. I still have a reason for being, with many reasons to be grateful—namely, my three surviving children—along with the promise of one day reuniting with loved ones who have passed on to the other side of this life.

I realized that not only did I have my three beautiful surviving children, I also had me. And I had a responsibility for the life that I had been given. I find comfort in knowing we do maintain some connection to our loved ones on the other side. Now Marshall's pain inspires me to help and encourage others to work through their pain, to never quit. His memory inspires me to live my best. Now life seems less about "arriving" and more about experiencing—living and being together, helping one another, carrying one another when needed, sharing in each other's burdens, offering hope along the journey. I look forward to being with Marshall again, one day. I am ready for when that day comes.

Until then, I choose to live and thrive as best I can. And I hope that by telling Marshall's story, others will recognize that those hopeless moments where one sees no way out are the very moments we are positioned for a coming breakthrough. That's the moment we must encourage one another to push through, because our miracle is within reach. We must never give up. There is always hope! When you feel hopeless, be inspired. Because it's upon these moments of unexpected possibilities from impossible situations that we can build our faith, that our personal constitution is strengthened, and that we can experience the supernatural.

Throughout all my doubts, questions, and pain, I have returned full circle. God is love. So powerful is this love, our most tragic, dark moments can become light and hope for ourselves and others. This dark world needs more of that powerful light. Let's be the light.

Let's love one another.

Marshall's 21st birthday, 7 months before he went to heaven

Marshall painted this during the last few weeks of his life.

Afterword

Innate in any survivor is self-reflection and blame. We spend countless hours wondering what more could or should have been done. As survivors, we go through self-recrimination, only to find ourselves at the same place, with the same unanswered questions, and the same solution: Acceptance. We simply are left with one solution and that is to accept their choice, knowing we'll never know the reasons why they chose the path they did. With suicide and Charming Impossibles, how can we truly ever fully understand? What I do know is, through it all, the most futile mistake I made was self-damnation and blame.

Throughout the days and grief-filled nights following Marshall's passing, I read through Marshall's phone text messages. Night after night, I'd sit straight up in bed in a panic, fretting, "If only I said this or shared that. . . ."

My grieving heart allowed me no rest, no peace, no restitution. The yearnings, the longings, the trying to imagine living without him seemed dauntingly intolerable.

This led to my calling Barry. I asked him to meet for lunch so that he could tell me everything he could remember about his two-hour conversation with Marshall.

Barry met me with a life-giving gift. He brought me a typed outline of his conversation with Marshall. Throughout the three hours we spent together, Barry referred to his outline diligently, assuring nothing was left unsaid from what he could remember. He expounded on how his and Marshall's experiences were similar, different, and unique. Still somewhat numbed by the trauma of loss, I listened, but the information was so precious, so much. My broken soul tried to absorb what it could but, eventually, my mind glazed over and began shutting down.

At home, I filed Barry's precious notes in Marshall's box of memorabilia. Weeks went by, and the "what ifs" kept piling up. The same thoughts kept returning. I became convinced that had I shared certain thoughts, Marshall would still be here. I was sure that if only he knew a certain "this or that," Marshall would be here. It was because of what wasn't said, I convinced myself, that Marshall was gone.

It was all about what I left unsaid.

One night, plagued by yet another haunting memory of what had not been said, I paced by Marshall's box and was reminded of Barry's notes. Frantically scrambling through the file for those notes, I discovered Marshall's notes from the Women's Center of Tarrant County next to Barry's outline.

I unfolded Barry's outline. Reading over every word, I learned Barry had gone over every single thought, idea, and scenario I had been beating myself up over . . . the things that I thought were left unsaid.

Then I turned to Marshall's notes from the Women's Center. In his own handwriting, he scripted his strengths, weaknesses, and knowledge of his personality type. The Women's Center covered everything I had hoped to cover when Marshall changed his mind and refused to spend the week with me.

He knew. He knew everything about himself I hoped he would know. He's the single- most sensitive and rare personality type. These people often feel alone in the world. They are deep thinkers and lovers. He learned these things about himself there. He learned that hurtful words affect his personality type more deeply than others. They covered everything I hoped to cover the week he was to spend with me. Between the Women's Center and Barry's notes, not one subject had been overlooked, not one thought unshared. Barry said it all. Holding those notes to my aching heart, I cried my first tears of relief. I finally allowed myself to stop blaming myself. I set myself free. Barry knew God sent him to Marshall. Barry told Marshall so. I believe that is true. If Marshall wouldn't listen to him, he wasn't going to listen to anyone. His mind was made up.

By sharing our story, I hope to bring peace and hope to the survivors still wrestling with if only. If onlys and should haves are not options.

Together, let's live our best. Accept other's choice. Choose self-acceptance.

Most importantly, choose life.

"I am the youngest of my family but am also the biggest. People seem to have always expected more from me because I am larger and stronger. I guess that makes me look older. But they also respect me more, too. Some guys would use that to run over others or take advantage of others. Kids can be pretty mean to each other. I have been treated that way myself by my own father. So, I try to do differently. I try to be nice to the kid everyone else makes fun of. I can without being teased because I am big and kids won't mess with me."

-Marshall

A Mother's Anguish

—Susan E Foster

From deep slumber, to straight up in my bed
Thinking he'd still be here if only this I said.
It's three o'clock in the morning
If only I *did* that, I think my son wouldn't be dead.

Pacing in stride throughout the house
To evidently falling fast asleep;
I process the dreaded "If only,"
Awakening to tears I can't keep.

The tears, they fall from my eyes
Before opening, not fully awake.
Tears also fall throughout the day
No matter how happy I fake.

Will this mother live beyond
Suicide at 21 years? It's too much.
You, God, allowed life challenges, too far.
Are you truly loving, good, and such?

Loving and faithful you claim, oh really?
What about this hell?
It's noon, tears freely flow without warning.
In turmoil, I reel darker still.

No luster left to life or purpose
Disappointed, my faith's but a shredding thread.
In what and in whom do I now believe
After my final drop has bled?

No longer do I want to be here . . . Oh, wait!
I have three beautiful surviving children,
For them, I must hope.
Dare I leave *them*? This I could never do . . . Nope!

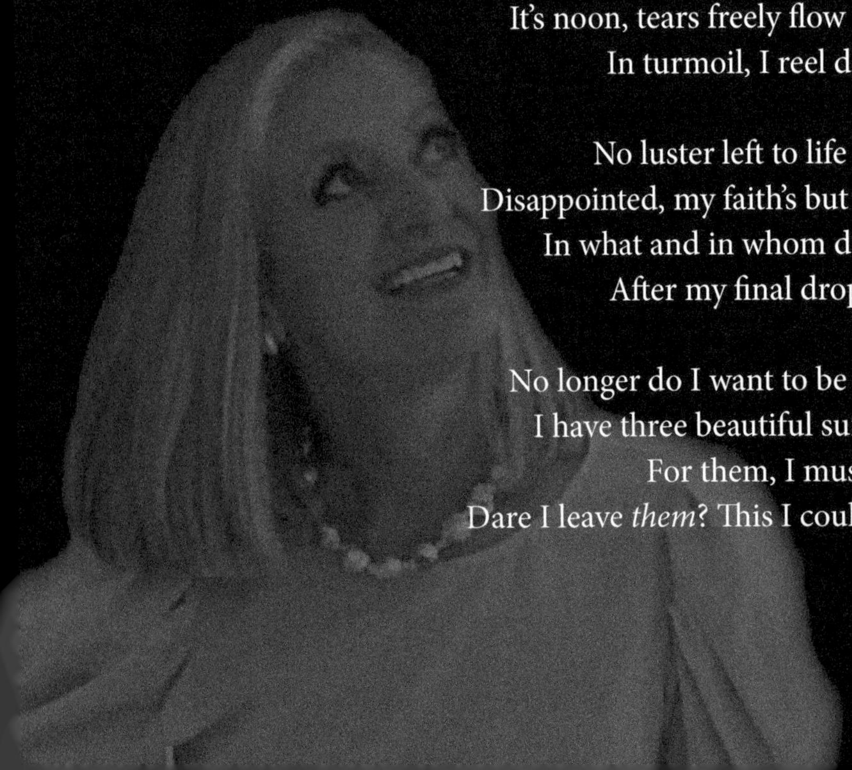

God has been faithful, loving and kind
With Barry, Ever, dear friends, and family.
God did reach out to my Marshall
Quitting and giving up, too? Not me!

God accompanied me deep in my valley,
And, on mountains with skies of blue.
In darkness, light and in between,
He remained the God I always knew.

In spite of doubt, blaming and self-pity
Emerge reason and purpose with joy.
This gift of life I shall continue
Until finished, I'll *will* to enjoy.

Looking forward to seeing my youngest son,
Together we'll watch his siblings from above.
Though through a connection, I feel he is here,
As we're forever intertwined through love.

Until the day we five are united again
God's comfort and love I accept.
I arise refined through this anguishing loss
though many tears I will have wept.

Life is not easy,
Nor is it a forever hell.
In both the good and bad
We must choose to respond well.

One day we'll be forever at peace
Where no evil will freely roam.
Together, in the hands of a loving God
Never again, alone.

Acknowledgments

The Marshall Racing Project 33 has been best described as an organic movement, due in large part to the fact that all involved were more drawn toward it, volunteering active participation, rather than being sought after. Each person involved joined as if attracted by a spiritual or soul magnet. Truly, I have never been part of anything quite like it. To me, it feels as though we have been chosen, almost like a "calling." What's fascinating is how utterly diverse and unique we all are. And yet we work together in seamless harmony, as though a conductor is orchestrating our ideas into beautiful music—in this case, in the form of a book.

My first book, *Charming Impossibles: How Ordinary Angels Help Free the Hopelessly Stuck*, launched in April of 2020 at the onset of COVID-19. With the completion of that project, space within my heart and soul opened to do more for those suffering exacerbated abuse due to the pandemic. Compounding my concern was the simultaneous rise of suicide rates among young people. Our hope is that Inside His locked Box: The Marshall Racing Project 33 will inspire hope, create positive change, and encourage faith in one another—Ordinary Angels are all around us. May each reader see Ordinary Angels along their own path, especially amidst life's darkest struggles.

For each important contribution to this book, I am most sincerely grateful. No litany of thanksgiving will ever be enough. The generosity of everyone involved is supernatural and it is quite humbling to accept each gift. I could never properly repay you all; you know who you are. While proper acknowledgment of so many Ordinary Angels is not possible on these pages, I must at least try with a certain few.

Ever Gomez, your magnificent transformation of Marshall's motorcycle, his lifelong dream, is a gift not only to my family but also to countless others. Thank you for your pure, selfless effort that allows Marshall's impact and memory to carry on. The way your racing team was prepared and already embracing the "newcomer" Marshall was the completion of his dream. He wanted a place to belong, a brotherhood of mentorship and fun. Had he accepted your gracious invitation, I am confident he would still be among us. Thank you Ever, Ruben, Eli, and David. What awaited Marshall in you is what I use to inspire others as Marshall's dream would have been fulfilled in becoming part of your team. You were what he wanted and needed. And you were available to him if only he had eyes to see. Your creation of The Marshall Racing Project 33 effects healing and hope, inspiring others to look for opportunities to be the change they long to see and to see the change that is already happening along their path. Thank you for your part in erasing stigma and shame from the issue of mental illness. Thank you for creating opportunities to ask, "How are you really doing?" Your story reinforces the fact that when one is at their very lowest, that's when their breakthrough is imminent. Your message encourages all of us to hold on and push through.

Thank you, Tara Sawyer Foundation for teaming up with Marshall Racing Project 33 Team to fund a scholarship in memory of Marshall. Your funds will help supply a training bike and the training expenses incurred. Once again, Ever, you and your team are reaching out to a young person much like Marshall. My heart smiles. I look forward to meeting the young people who will come forward to benefit in Marshall's stead with your team.

Barry King, within minutes of meeting you, I was asking you to visit my emotionally troubled son. Saying yes to me required bravery, vulnerability, and came with potential risk. You did for Marshall what he did for others. While still working through your own pain, you reached out to him. If any action or words could have gotten through to him at that time, it was yours. You have been integral to my own acceptance, healing, and peace. Thank you for the inspiration and example you have become for me and many others.

Mary Ann Contreras, you supported Marshall as he fretted about paying off *every* medical bill after his accident and provided him a meaningful opportunity to publicly testify about his miraculous recovery and his experience of exceptional care within the award winning, JPS Level 1 Trauma Center. You showed Marshall how he could effect positive change from his pain . . . and that such pain was not in vain. Thank you for standing by Marshall, for believing in him, and for being his and our family friend.

Michelle Vardeman Martin, when you finished reading my book, *Charming Impossibles,* you called asking how you could be an Ordinary Angel. You were a voice from 38 years ago. Never would I have known 38 years ago that two young girls encountering each other through high school activities, I would later be so greatly impacted by our friendship. Once you offered your editorial talents on future projects, I knew Marshall's dream to write a book would be realized. Your phone call and belief in this project impacted my decision to take this on more than any other influence. Without that phone call, I'm doubtful I would have taken on the task of publishing *Inside His locked Box.* I feel so proud to publish Marshall's writing—it was a big dream of his, and so it is mine as well. I will always consider this project one of, if not the, most important professional accomplishments of my life. To you, for this gift, I will remain eternally grateful.

To my four children, you will forever be the why for what I do. I love you.

There are countless others who have stood by us, supported us, sacrificed for us, and given to us. We are aware of you, grateful to you, and ask God's blessing upon you.

About Susan E Foster

Susan E Foster is a mother, author, speaker, coach, and advocate hoping to equip men, women, and children to recognize the abusive *Charming Impossibles* in their lives. By sharing her personal story of survival and faith in her first two books, *Charming Impossibles: How Ordinary Angels Help Free the Hopelessly Stuck* and *Inside His locked Box: The Marshall Racing Project 33 Story,* Susan reveals how the oftentimes deadly web of confusion is spun around abuse. Susan is committed to inspire healthy change for survivors to help them overcome and heal.

A graduate of the University of Texas School of Journalism, Susan writes compelling narratives of hope from extraordinary deeds of ordinary people hoping readers discover the Ordinary Angels in their own lives. Susan E Foster resides in Fort Worth, Texas.

MARSHALL RACING
PROJECT 33

Foundations

Marshall Racing Project 33 (MRP33)

ABOUT: Marshall Racing Project 33 is designed to empower individuals to talk openly about mental health issues, recognize symptoms, utilize local resources, and seek help. By raising awareness on the topic of suicide and providing access to local resources, we aim to inspire wellness, reduce stigma, and prevent suicide. Recovery is possible and help is available. Together we can make a difference in the lives of individuals experiencing mental health challenges by offering support and providing opportunities.

OUR MISSION: Our mission is to promote Mental Health Awareness, and to shine a light on Suicide Prevention to the communities we serve.

OUR VISION: Our vision is to eradicate the silence and stigma associated with suicide and promote a community that is healthy and safe.

To learn more, please visit www.mrp33.org.

From left to right: Ruben Perez, Eli Gaucin, Ever Gomez, and David Lisboa

RPM
RUBEN PEREZ MOTORWORKS
Marshall Racing Project

33
Kawasaki
Ninja
VORTEX
RPM
Marshall Racing Project

Proceeds from Your Purchase of This Book Support These Foundations

Hope Squads reduce youth suicide through education, training, and peer intervention. Hope Squad members are nominated by their peers and trained by advisors. They strive to create a safe school environment, promote connectedness, support antibullying, encourage mental wellness, reduce mental health stigma, and prevent substance misuse. Please visit www.hopesquad.com or call 801.342.3447 for more information.

Our mission at the **Jordan Harris Foundation** is to eradicate suicide by funding depression research, creating awareness through education, erasing the stigma, and providing hope to those who are struggling in silence. Please visit www.jordanharrisfoundation.org for more information.

JPS Health Network is a $950 million, tax-supported health care system for Tarrant County in North Texas. Anchored by a 537-bed acute care hospital, the network includes more than 46 community-based clinics, including 20 school-based clinics. John Peter Smith Hospital is home to Tarrant County's first and only Level 1 Trauma Center, its only psychiatric emergency services site, and has the largest family medicine residency program in the nation. Our network employs more than 6,500 plus people. Please visit www.jpshealthnet.org/ for more information.

JPS Health Network was named the best hospital in the United States, according to a new hospital evaluating system unveiled Tuesday by *Washington Monthly Magazine*. Ranking near the top of every category, it out-scored the most prestigious healthcare organizations in America. July, 2020

Tara Sawyer Foundation

Jonell, Susan, and Gina

TARA SAWYER FOUNDATION
ALEX CHANCE SCHOLARSHIP

TSF
TARA SAWYER FOUNDATION

MARSHALL RACING
PROJECT 33 SCHOLARSHIP
SPONSORED BY
TARA SAWYER FOUNDATION

"A good friend knows all your best stories,
but a best friend has lived them with you."
—Unknown

"Friendship isn't about who you've known the longest.
It's about who came, and never left your side."
—Unknown

"You are not my friend, you are my sister."
—Susan E Foster

Friendship: A Legacy of Light from Three Mothers' Darkest Pain

—Susan E Foster

There is a supernatural energy shift that occurs when girlfriends come together. Life alters and makes way for our power when we unite. Together, we problem-solve. When it's for one of our own, we move mountains. That's what began to happen when I awakened the first morning of leading my four teenagers out of domestic abuse into the great unknown.

With the morning dew and sunrise returned the looming fear. With my head still on the pillow, lying in bed upstairs in my brother's home, looking up at the ceiling, wondering how to face the first day of our new life, I was bombarded with a list of issues needing immediate attention. I was contemplating the many needs of my four teen-agers: *What do I tackle first?*

Suddenly, the doorbell rings and I hear my sister-in-law greet a familiar voice. Walking down the stairs, I saw a great big bright-eyed smile on Gina's beautiful face. My best friend since the age of 12, Gina, was standing at the foot of the stairs holding three steaming to-go cups of coffee, smiling. "I thought you might like a fresh Starbucks," she said, adding, "Welcome home!"

Home . . . I *was* home, in my hometown where I had family and hometown friends. I had not felt home since I married. The *me* they knew had become someone in my past life. It felt good, soothing, to be with people who knew the *me* I lost. They knew me before all my marital trauma began. Their parents were friends of my parents; they not only watched me grow up, they watched my brother. There stood my lifelong best friend, one who knew when

I wasn't being myself. Oh yes, she could see through any imitation. She knew me.

"Susan, we hear this new husband of yours coming out of your mouth," my true friends warned me as an engaged young 23-year-old girl about to marry. "You don't even sound like yourself anymore," they'd implore with worry. "You don't dress or act like yourself, either," they'd boldly say.

"It's the *improved* me," I defended as I was fast becoming convinced. I had no idea the danger of naiveté. What I thought was virtuous was, in fact, my folly almost to my total destruction.

We were two of a group of soul mate friendships, some of which went back to third grade and beyond. We went through the adolescent stage, the disco dancing, and what was supposed to be *fun* "Teen Dance Nights." Gina could move to the groove of the *Saturday Night Fever* soundtrack. I, on the other hand, was ridiculously stiff and awkward, turning down any invite to the dance floor, watching her blissfully twist and twirl from the sidelines.

Determined that would never happen again, Gina stood me before her mirror with the Saturday Night Fever record playing, teaching me all her great moves in the privacy of her bedroom. The next Teen Night Dance, I was out on that floor. If she had a finger pointed up in the air with a hip swung out, I did too; if she twirled, I twirled, and we laughed hysterically at each other as I finally learned to make it out on the dance floor on my own.

Fast forward past all our weddings, and into motherhood came the crises that rocked all our worlds. Gina's 10-year-old daughter, Tara, contracted an amoeba-borne illness while swimming in a lake.

Nothing prepares a parent for the loss of a child, nor friends on how to console one so brokenhearted. Our friend group rallied around Gina, consoling her, sharing her grief and tears, totally unsure of what to say. How does one console the yearning heart of mother for her child? Gina had always been our leader. She organized our first pep squad, served in almost every student leader position, excelled in academics and sports. Now she would lead us in dealing with a mother's greatest loss.

Not sure how I could be a support for her, during a momentary break of our deep, communal rushing flow of sobs I risked asking an apparently unthinkable question: "What are you going to wear to the service?" Four wide-eyed sets of eyes looked at me shocked and appalled, as if to say in disgust, "*Susan?* Seriously, you're asking this *now*?"

"Well," I said, having started it, "what look shall we go for?" running with the question I always asked her for any and every event. Bringing our normalcy to this traumatic moment would either feel good or really bad. Knowing this was going to be the most crowded funeral service I'd ever attend, I waited for her to respond. Shaking her head, cracking her first smile, Gina breaks the gasping in of air with, "Susan, you know me so well."

Temporarily tossing the mascara-laden tissues to the trash, we all pile in a car to take Gina shopping. *Sometimes, the answer is a new pair of shoes* has long been my personal mantra, and I continue to stand by it today. Bombarding a local boutique, we five usher our friend cloaked in the balm of "grief shock" that numbs the coming flood of unbearable pain to find that perfectly put-together outfit.

Tara's funeral left us forever altered. It was our first loss of that magnitude. The loss of a child is a loss all its own. It was deep. It was dark. It didn't leave. Not for a long, long time.

In grief counseling, Gina later learned that when life's path takes you on a sudden drop into a dark, deep abyss, not all your friends meet you down there. Oftentimes, the ones you least expect are there to greet you, softening the blow, while others stay at the top looking down, just waiting for you to come back up. Sometimes, you are never able to make it back to them.

A crisis comes in many layers. It either attracts or repels the people you love. The pain is multilayered as well, because every kind of loss involves more than just one person. Even within our group, some of us picked up where others dropped off.

It happens.

* * *

January 2, 2010, almost three months before my children and I packed up to leave, my other very best friend since the third grade rushed us back into the next of our greatest crises.

Jonell was the friend that would say, "We're going to do *what*?" when presented with one of my wild, exciting adventurous ideas to which all my other friends, possessing too much common sense, would boldly refuse. Jonell, however, was the one upon whom I could always rely. She faithfully joined me on many escapades, exploring many outlandish ideas, including an exciting high school senior trip to go on a road trip without a plan. No matter how unsound my idea, I could always rely upon her resounding "Okay." She was always game for every crazy idea I pitched her way.

"Let's just take off without telling our parents and see where our adventure leads!" was my bright idea for two young teens, never giving the question of safety nor our parents' emotional turmoil a single thought leading us on an extended weekend adventure to Galveston Beach with fake I.D.'s. Fortunately, an Ordinary Angel swept in, diverting a few episodes of what could have turned terribly dark resulting in dreamy teen romance novel material.

Needless to say, we came home from that trip in deep trouble with our parents. Their anger quickly softened when they heard all about our adventures . . . who we met, our experiences on a private boat excursion, and our safe stay in a boy's family mansion, where we were served brunch on crystal and china before saying our final farewells.

Eight years after Tara's passing, and three months before my crisis of fleeing abuse was in full bloom, our second daughter of the group went to heaven at the precious young age of 15. What started as aches and pains in her wrists and ankles turned into fainting spells, visits to multiple children's hospitals, and more and more blood work, with no conclusive answers to the cause. This was Alex, Jonell's otherwise healthy, vibrant, sassy little high-school teenaged soccer player, the baby of the family.

There Alex lay in the same ICU as Tara once had. Visiting Alex was Gina's first time to return since the passing of Tara. And going down the familiar corridor brought forth daunting, challenging, ever-raw stuffed memories. As she forged ahead to support Jonell, our friend who was no stranger to life trauma, I worried about both of them pulling out of this one. Jonell survived losing her mother at the age of eight; being shunned by her cantankerous, crusty, harsh father; divorcing from a tumultuous marriage with four little girls, and now add *this*?

Her list of traumas, at the time, included all that we had collectively been through and more. With Hollywood beauty and Diana-like grace, she faced her life from the outside-in, looking like a beauty queen on the outside while fighting vicious depression within. Losing Alex would take her depression to new heights.

Our hope rested in her wonderful, amazing second husband, David, whom she and we all love and appreciate. It would be a heavy load for him, but we would be there to support him as he carried the mother lode. It would take her family, all of us, shock therapy, psychotherapy, medication changes, drinking with her, overlooking her drinking alone, girls trips, and, of course, *shopping* to see her through. Nothing was too much for us. We took turns with each other through the ugly. Infidelity, financial crises, and more couldn't break the bond of our friendships; in fact, it made us stronger.

Crowded around Alex's graveside, huddling and hugging beneath a cold, overcast Texas January gray sky, another storm cloud loomed, threatening to erupt. Lost in grief with and for Jonell, Gina whispered to me, "Susan, I don't know what to say," allowing a different set of tears to flow freely down her cheeks. "I'm scared for you to return to him," she added, expressing herself more boldly in response to the massive hematoma covering my shin beneath my pant leg.

Knowing my husband recently kicked me, again, she begged, "Please stay here," as they all turned toward me in unison.

"I drank the juice," I responded. "I let all this happen. It's all on me. I have been so stupidly blind, believing all his fundamentalist lies, and I must fully own this predicament I'm in.

"Please don't bother Jonell with this," I asked of them all. "Please take good care of her, because I can't. I'll figure something out for me," I said, assuring them. "I am going back for my kids. I'll figure a way out."

Walking away from my trusted group of friends shrouded in grief, tears, and fear for two of their own, I could see Jonell in the distance, hovering over her daughter's white casket, offering a final hug. From the grassy, crowded hillside of mourners in black, I drove myself back to what would be my closest encounter with hell.

Not even three full months later, on April 2, 2010, I awaken in my brother's home to find Gina greeting me at the foot of the stairs.

How is it that so many memories flash through our minds in seconds? Carefully taking a cup of steaming coffee from Gina, I held and hugged my dear, precious friend. This was my *girlfriend* who I was bonded to like a sister all my life and continues to today. . . .

At that time, The Tara Sawyer Foundation provided my children's school uniforms, affording my children to complete their final couple months of the school year with their cousin in his church school. Gina's family foundation, The Tara Sawyer Foundation, was formed after the tragic loss of her 10-year-old daughter, Tara. Gina and her family turned their tragedy into an opportunity to help others.

Life has a way of circling around. Her tragedy helped me then. I could hardly believe it was happening. *We* are *doing this,* I remember thinking at the time, *We are going to survive this abuse.* With the help of *sister-friends,* I was beginning to believe I could lead my children out of abuse into a healthy future.

Seven years later, my children and I *were* making it until my youngest son, Marshall, began to spiral downward emotionally. On October 12, 2017, my 21-year-old son committed suicide following his miraculous survival of a harrowing motorcycle accident. It was not the accident that led him to end his life. It goes much deeper. Marshall was battling thoughts of suicide long before the crash. The full story is in my first book, *Charming Impossibles: How Ordinary Angels Help Free the Hopelessly Stuck.* Readers will learn how "Ordinary Angels" became a beacon of hope for me, my three surviving children, and many others.

In my second book, *Inside His locked Box: The Marshall Racing Project 33 Story,* I give voice to Marshall. Through Marshall's personal inspiring writing intertwined with the telling of our story, Inside His locked Box is a message that breakthrough is imminent the more hopeless we become. Through this inside look into Marshall's troubled written struggles, his awaiting breakthrough is discovered. And it was available to him if only he had eyes to see. Marshall experienced perhaps his greatest sense of joy, accomplishment, and independence on the seat of his motorcycle, a black Kawasaki Ninja. It was so much more than a motorcycle. It was his dream realized.

Through sharing our story, I hope readers will discover the Ordinary Angels in their own life, that there is always hope, and that breakthroughs are imminent especially at our darkest hours. At those moments, we simply must help each other hold on.

* * *

Facing the daunting challenge of losing the third child of our friendship group, "money seeds" from our supporting friends inspired The Tara Sawyer Foundation to, once again, create light and hope from pain by establishing The Alex Chance Scholarship and The Marshall Racing Project 33 Scholarship connecting our beloved children and our friendships in this meaningful memorial legacy of hope and love.

Thank you to Mary Ellen for planting seed money that gave birth to this vision.

To learn more, visit www.Tarasawyer.org and www.MRP33.org.

* * *

Susan E Foster is a mother, author, speaker, coach, and advocate hoping to equip men and women to recognize the abusive "Charming Impossibles" in their lives. By sharing her personal story of survival and faith, Susan reveals how we must never give up. She also detangles the web of confusion spun around abuse and works to inspire healthy change for men, women, and children to help them overcome and heal.

For more information, visit Susanefoster.com.

For all loved ones gone too soon and

In Loving Memory of

John Marshall Foster

…May you ride forever with the angels…

You will forever shine bright
in our memories of you…

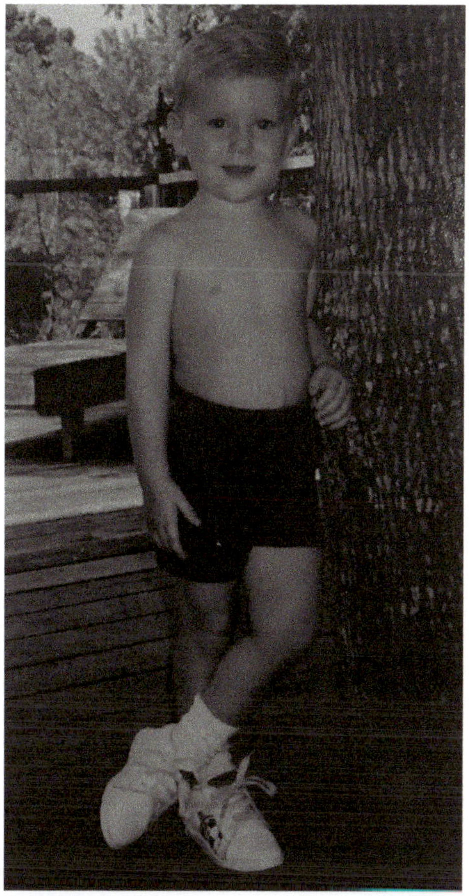

Marshall's 21st birthday family ski trip.

40¢
Sprite
40¢
RED FLASH

Notes

Foreword

1. United Health Foundation Annual Report (2020), "About Suicide," America's Health Rankings, https://www.americashealthrankings.org/explore/annual/measure/Suicide/state/ALL.

PART I

1. Beth Martens, *Journey: A Map of Archetypes to Find Lost Purpose in a Sea of Meaninglessness* (Santa Barbara, CA: Woodbridge Press Publishing Company, 2020), Kindle.
2. Ibid.
3. M. E. Thomas, *Confessions of a Sociopath: A Life Spent Hiding in Plain Sight* (New York: Broadway Books, 2014), 18. 102, 107.
4. See Katie Hurley, "ADHD & Anxiety in Children," Psycom, https://www.psycom. net/adhd-children-anxiety.

PART II

1."Key Injury and Violence Data," Centers for Disease Control and Prevention, https://www.cdc.gov/injury/wisqars/overview/key_data.html#:~:text=In%20the%20first%20half%20of,death%20among%20persons%201%2D44.
2. Larry M Gentilello, Dennis M. Donovan, Christopher W. Dunn, and Frederick P. Rivara, "Alcohol Interventions in Trauma Centers: Current Practice and Future Directions," JAMA,1995;274(13):1043–1048. doi:10.1001/jama.1995.03530130049027.
3. "Save Lives and Money," Safe States Alliance, https://cdn.ymaws.com/www.safestates.org/resource/resmgr/policy/Save_Lives_and_Money_FINAL.pdf.
4. Tracy Maness, "Suicide second leading cause of death for Texas youth," *Chron.*, March 8, 2019, https://www.chron.com/neighborhood/bellaire/news/article/Suicide-second-leading-cause-of-death-for-Texas-13673952.php.
5. Ibid.
6. Martens, *Journey*. Kindle.
7. Bruce Wilkinson, *The Dream Giver* (Colorado Springs, CO: Multnomah, 2003), 27.
8. Michael D. De Bellis and Abigail Zisk, "The Biological Effects of Childhood Trauma," *Child and Adolescent Psychiatric Clinics of North America*, Vol. 23, Issue 2,

2014, Pages 185-222, ISSN 1056-4993, ISBN 9780323289917, https://doi.org/10.1016/j.chc.2014.01.002. (https://www.sciencedirect.com/science/article/pii/S1056499314000030).

PART III

1. Billy Graham, *Hope for Each Day* (Nashville, TN: Thomas Nelson, 2012), 345.